W9-AWZ-972

"Shame cannot tolerate the real you who, armed with God's power, boldly faces the truth..."

Praise for *Th*

"Many of us are seeking ways to live he
around us, and in our relationships. Thr
of You, Dr. Alison Cook leads us to ask i
key strategies so the best of who God
develop. The path toward this kind of hea
I hope you will let this beautiful and tran

—LYSA TERKEURS
AUTHOR AND PRES

"*The Best of You* is a beautiful gift to ev
live from her true self. With wisdom dra
and years of clinical experience, Dr. Alis
ten to our divine inner wisdom, to see o
into relationships and communication th
practical guide to authentic living will be
everywhere!"

—JENNA RIEM
BESTSELL

"*The Best of You* is like therapy in a book.
tions we all ask with nuance and grace. She
of painful relationship patterns and provi
relatable stories, reflection questions, and
conversations. This book is a must-read f
growth."

—JESSICA HONEGGER, FOUI
AND A

"With wisdom and tender strength, Dr. Alisc
will empower us to live from the best and t
selves. *The Best of You* is a phenomenal resour
psychology, and Dr. Cook's own hard-earned
for this important offering, and I will be reco

—AUNDI KOLBER, THERAPIS

"In *The Bes*
how to do t
deepest self,
the painful e
break free a
daughter of
you how to
lead, you wi

—BE
BES

"Alison's br
of the true
a giant lea
helpful and

—CH

"It require
It requires
become a
is as acces
of these t
that empe
ingesting
embodies
with so n
you are re

"In *The I*
often he
awarene
what I ca
but Dr.

—J. S.

"Not only does Dr. Cook marry psychology and spirituality in a synchronized dance in *The Best of You*, but she does so with unpretentious simplicity—reminding us that wisdom at its best is wisdom accessible to all. She is gifted in breaking concepts down with everyday examples to help the reader feel more confident in both understanding and applying them in their daily lives. As I read *The Best of You*, I was struck by how it wasn't just informative but also facilitated an experience of connecting with my own sense of self and deepening this connection."

—Dr. Jean Cheng, clinical psychologist at Talitha Koum Psychology and creator of the Instagram @jeanpsychologist

"Dr. Alison is a bold and courageous messenger for today's Christian woman. She exposes toxic teaching that keeps women feeling small, dependent, passive, and silent. *The Best of You* is a practical, Biblical road map for a woman to break free from who she thinks, feels, or has been told she is, and take steps to grow into who God created her to be."

—Leslie Vernick, international speaker, relationship coach, and author of seven books including the bestselling *The Emotionally Destructive Marriage*

"Dr. Alison Cook brilliantly yet practically identifies common misconceptions in our relationships, including our relationship with God. *The Best of You* weaves together psychology and theology in a profoundly prophetic way, leading us toward the gift God has provided since the days in the garden of Eden—redemption. Dr. Cook gives us the best of herself as a gentle guide and trusted companion."

—Monique S. Gadson, PhD, LPC therapist, and assistant professor of Counseling Psychology at The Seattle School of Theology & Psychology

"*The Best of You* is a nuanced and relatable guide to healing, health, and wholeness, while also serving as an antidote to the quick fix, empty promises that have left us feeling frustrated, lonely, and doubting ourselves. Each chapter invites us to unpack and unlearn the toxic narratives and beliefs around the intersection of our faith, relationships, and our sense of self in a way that helps reclaim the best of who we are as we show up in all areas of our lives."

—Rebecca Ching, LMFT, psychotherapist, leadership developer, and podcast host of *The Unburdened Leader*

"God created you with an enduring capacity to emanate love within yourself such that mercy and grace spill over into the world around you. In this engaging book my friend, Alison, skillfully invites you to discover and explore a life shaped by this spiritual practice. I'm excited for you to dive into these chapters, breathe deeply as you ponder the possibilities, and transform more and more into the person you most want to be."

—KIMBERLY MILLER, MTh, LICENSED MARRIAGE AND FAMILY THERAPIST, AND COAUTHOR OF *BOUNDARIES FOR YOUR SOUL*

"In the warm and kind style she is known for, Dr. Alison Cook invites you to embrace and accept what can feel elusive and unattainable about changing old ways of relating. In *The Best of You*, she asks—and answers—the questions you have about what holds you back from becoming who you were meant to be and who you already are inside."

—TAMMY SOLLENBERGER, AUTHOR OF *THE ONE INSIDE* AND HOST OF *THE ONE INSIDE* PODCAST

From Dr. Alison's Weekly Email Readers

"I absolutely loved this book! Delving into each chapter felt like an emotional healing balm." —TANYA F.

"This book is both validating and transformative." —CHEYENNE L.

"*The Best of You* has shown me a new angle on setting boundaries and building healthy connections." —TABITHA S.

"I am super grateful that this book came into this current season of my life—it is a great resource that is helping me connect to God more authentically and be a good friend for myself again!" —LIYUAN P.

"I thoroughly enjoyed reading *The Best of You*. It is both honest and insightful with practical advice and helpful applications." —RACHEL P.

"I especially enjoy the powerful questions throughout the book, culminating in probing questions at each chapter's end. In a simple and clear way, this is the handbook Christian women are looking for both to improve and heal their lives!" —ANGELA W.

the best of you

Break Free from Painful Patterns,
Mend Your Past, and Discover
Your True Self in God

Dr. Alison Cook

NELSON
BOOKS

An Imprint of Thomas Nelson

Published in Nashville, Tennessee, by Nelson Books, an imprint of Thomas Nelson. Nelson Books and Thomas Nelson are registered trademarks of HarperCollins Christian Publishing, Inc.

The author is represented by Alive Literary Agency, www.aliveliterary.com.

Thomas Nelson titles may be purchased in bulk for educational, business, fundraising, or sales promotional use. For information, please email SpecialMarkets@ThomasNelson.com.

Library of Congress Cataloging-in-Publication Data

Names: Cook, Allison, (Dr.), 1973- author.
Title: The best of you: break free from painful patterns, mend your past, and discover your true self in God / Dr. Allison Cook.
Description: Nashville: Thomas Nelson, 2022. | Includes bibliographical references. | Summary: "Dr. Alison Cook delivers life-changing strategies for helping women develop their voices, forge healthy relationships, and embrace the holy, sacred work of becoming their true selves in God"-- Provided by publisher.
Identifiers: LCCN 2022014537 (print) | LCCN 2022014538 (ebook) | ISBN 9781400234547 (hardcover) | ISBN 9781400234554 (ebook)
Subjects: LCSH: Christian women--Religious life. | Self-actualization (Psychology)--Religious aspects--Christianity. | Self-actualization (Psychology) in women.
Classification: LCC BV4527 .C6565 2022 (print) | LCC BV4527 (ebook) | DDC 248.8/43--dc23/eng/20220411
LC record available at https://lccn.loc.gov/2022014537
LC ebook record available at https://lccn.loc.gov/2022014538

Printed in the United States of America

22 23 24 25 26 LSC 10 9 8 7 6 5 4 3 2 1

To you, dear reader.
May you be free of past pain.
May you continue to mend.
May you discover the best that's yet to come.

Contents

Contents

Part 3: Express the Best of You

Part 4: Live the Best of You

Introduction

THE BEST OF YOU ALMOST DIDN'T MAKE IT INTO BEING. AS A clinician, I had longed for an accessible, practical guide that laid out key elements of how we heal—a sort of "therapy in a book" that brings together the best of faith with the best of psychology in a way that speaks especially to the unique needs of women.

But at the exact moment I began to bring this book to life, I encountered a trauma that would literally knock me off my feet, forcing me to test everything I hoped to write about.

It was a *Friday Night Lights* kind of night—a crisp September evening in the football-loving town of Sheridan, Wyoming. After six months of lockdown with our two college-aged, remote-learning kids, I was getting ready for a quarantine-style date night with my husband: a country road tailgate dinner, complete with takeout from a favorite restaurant eaten under the stars. Eager to get dressed up for the first time in forever, I headed into our bathroom to put on some makeup. As I pumped concealer onto my finger, I noticed something strange: it was as if my finger was completely disconnected from my body. Prepped for the seemingly simple task of gliding over to my face, this finger was stubbornly refusing all my mental efforts to move it.

In a matter of moments, a body I had for the most part trusted to perform basic tasks was suddenly completely unresponsive to me. As hard as I tried, I could not move that finger. I felt as powerless as if I were trying to use my mind to transport a book across the room by staring at it.

Ironically, the day before, I had sent out a blog post on learning to trust yourself. A therapist for nearly two decades, I had started writing out observations from my work. In two years my blog had grown to more than thirty thousand readers. That responsibility instilled a sense of fear and trembling in me as I pressed Send each week. In this particular post, I had been able to put words to something that I had wrestled with for decades:

> If you are never taught how to develop—and trust—your own sense of self, you have no choice but to blindly trust other people. How can you possibly forge healthy relationships with others—if you don't first understand how to show up as the person God made *you* to be?

As I wrote, my usually busy mind had felt oddly calm, as if the letters had taken on a life of their own and dropped onto my screen one by one, crystallizing years of personal struggle and professional pondering.

I had nurtured a deep faith in God in college, a formative move on my not-so-faith-filled Ivy League campus. But I somehow managed to remain completely disconnected from my own sense of self—descending into a decade of self-doubt and chronic people pleasing. I didn't lose my faith in God as my life slowly unraveled; I lost faith in *myself.*

It took a PhD in both religion and psychology—combined with a midlife meltdown—to dig myself out. And this blog post was a culmination of reflections on what I had observed in my own life and in the lives of the women who had come to me for counseling. *This is the exact message I have to give,* I thought. *We have to develop a deep connection to our own sense of self—work that goes hand in hand with trusting the One who made us.*

Developing a strong sense of self is paramount to living the life God has for us. It's essential to healthy relationships with other people. It involves a deep understanding of your strengths, needs, values, and purpose. It's finding—and expressing—your unique voice in all kinds of relationships and situations. It's trusting that you have what it takes to meet the challenges you will face, no matter what life throws your way.

My message had never felt so clear. After I hit Send and shut down my laptop, I'd had the profound feeling that a disconnect deep inside me had finally reached its end. Now, as I stood in front of the mirror not twenty-four hours later, I was trying to make sense of another disconnect I could not have possibly predicted. My finger simply would not move.

Is it asleep? I wondered fleetingly, searching for a familiar category to describe what was happening. *No, this is not that.*

I began to register a terrifying observation: *My finger is no longer responding to the cues my brain is sending it.*

And I started screaming for my husband. *"Joe!"* I yelled, holding the unresponsive finger out in front of me. *"Joe!"*

As Joe rushed in, I tried to explain what was happening. I could hear my words slurring, like they were coming out in slow motion, and I started staggering as if I was drunk. It was suddenly no longer only my finger that had disconnected; it was my hand, my arm . . . and just like that the whole left side of my body. I was on the floor when we both realized what was happening. Only in my forties, with no known medical conditions, I was having a stroke. While I had been laboring over my blog post only one day prior, a blood clot was making its way to my brain.

My husband rushed me to the emergency room where doctors went into action and immediately worked to mitigate the damage of the clot. Three days later, I was able to walk out of the hospital, my body relatively unscathed. But my heart and my soul would forever be changed. The terror of that moment evoked understandable anxiety, and I found myself traveling down an unwanted path through shock, fear, and bargaining that I had so often accompanied my clients on. I had to surrender, in a whole new way, to a process of healing from the emotional aftermath of trauma.

The irony was not lost on me. Suddenly I entered a poignant season of practicing everything I taught. Each day I would find ways to gently soothe my anxious mind, noticing and moving toward what brought glimmers of relief. I honored the tears that showed up, often in the middle of the night. I leaned in to loving relationships, the presence of which was a marvel to me after years of healing my own painful patterns of relating to other people.

And I talked with God honestly instead of hiding doubts, fears, and even anger. One sunny afternoon, a few months after the stroke, I found myself alone in the middle of a hayfield as my husband fly-fished nearby. I looked up into the enormous blue sky encased on all sides with golden yellow and asked, *What is it that you want me to do with this life you have given me? You certainly have my attention.*

And, as is God's way, I sensed not an easy answer but a loving nudge in a new but also strangely familiar direction, where God asked me questions: *What is it that you want to do with this life you've been given? I know you. I see you. I want you to use the gifts you've been given.*

I wanted to write *The Best of You.*

This book you are reading is my answer to God's question. What I want at the core of my being is to teach you how to do the hard, beautiful work of becoming—and trusting—your truest, deepest self, in partnership with the God who made you.

You may not have had a life-threatening stroke that brought you to a place of examining what to do when life gets the best of you. But I have no doubt you've had pain. You've suffered through loneliness, loss, self-doubt, or betrayal.

You've no doubt asked God, "What is it that you want from me in this crisis, this relationship, this heartache, this *life*?" You've no doubt begged God to show you the way forward, the way out of the struggle you are facing.

The problem is that healing—whether it's current heartaches or past wounds—is rarely a one-time event. Healing is a process, a practice, a way of becoming more of who you really are. It's the work every single one of us has been given to do. It's the work that I believe is at the center of God's heart. Healing starts within us and flows out to our loved ones, our neighbors, and our world.

I'm not here to give you easy answers. I don't presume to understand the sometimes strange ways of God. But I do know that whatever you are facing, you have one of two choices. You can turn toward the work of healing this beautiful life you've been given, or you can turn away.

You can turn toward the question I believe God is asking each and every one of us: *What is it that you want to do with this life you've been given? I'm listening.*

PART 1

Uncover the Hidden You

Over the years, I have come to realize that the greatest trap in our life is not success, popularity, or power, but self-rejection.

—HENRI NOUWEN, *YOU ARE THE BELOVED*

Chapter 1

What Do You Want?

A Brave New Direction

I KNOW YOU HAVE PAIN.

You might feel paralyzed by an overwhelming set of circumstances, a difficult relationship, or an impossible decision. Parts of you are aching inside, and you long to know how to fix what is wrong. You feel disheartened, doubtful, and desperate for answers.

Maybe you've agonized over whether to cut ties with someone or stay involved a little while longer. It might be a soured friendship, an arrogant colleague, or a toxic family member. Or maybe you're exhausted by the busyness of life, struggling with loneliness, or feeling anxious. It might involve a parenting challenge, an unexpected transition, or a job you need but also hate. You may be wondering, *How did that person or situation get the best of me?*

Whatever your situation may be, it consumes your thoughts, heart, and prayer time. You may have tried to process it with a counselor, asked a friend for help, or silently begged God to take the pain away;

but you stay stuck, feeling trapped in a cycle of analysis, self-doubt, and sometimes even self-blame.

Depending on the problem at hand, you may have asked yourself—and everyone around you—questions like these:

- *Am I a doormat if I stay involved?*
- *Does walking away make me selfish?*
- *What will happen if I stand up for myself?*
- *Do I have what it takes to make a change?*
- *Could someone please tell me what to do?*

When answers to these questions fail to appear, you become increasingly frustrated, exhausted, and overwhelmed. You suffer in silence, numb yourself to escape the pain, or muscle your way through until you quietly break.

I've been there too.

Like many women, I had no idea how to get the life or relationships I wanted. I trusted God, but I didn't understand what it meant to become the wholehearted person God made. I didn't know I could develop what psychologists call *agency*—that I could heal, grow in assertiveness, and develop a strong sense of self. Instead, I second-guessed every thought, feeling, or longing inside of me. It felt wrong to listen to, let alone trust, my own instincts.

When it came to the dilemmas I faced, I would do one of three things:

1. Pray for God to "tell me" the answers.
2. Analyze ad nauseam.
3. Seek out other people with strong opinions.

The result? Mostly I stayed stuck. I sabotaged opportunities for happiness and shied away from owning my own perspective, desires, and needs. Inside, I was trapped in fear, loneliness, and uncertainty. On the outside, I focused on making *other people* happy.

Maintaining this divide nearly shattered me—until one day I had a subtle but profound breakthrough. Desperate to relieve my growing anxiety, I found myself asking a critical question: *What do* I *want?*

All my efforts to focus on others had failed to address the turmoil inside me. But as I slowly started to pay attention to my own inner longings, no matter how simple or sometimes surprising, I sensed a bit of relief. Increasingly, I began to move toward these longings, one brave step at a time. Soon I was moving out of my trap and into a life I wanted. The question "What do *I* want?" seemed so simple yet so transformative. Why hadn't I considered it before?

I have seen a similar pattern over and over in my work as a counselor for two decades. As I listen to the details of a client's painful story unfold, I hear pain, guilt, and anger. I hear confusion, worry, and fear. I hear loneliness, grief, and frustration. And I hear a lot of ideas about what *other people* think:

- My friends think I need better boundaries.
- My mom thinks I should pray more.
- My partner is sick of hearing about it.

I listen. I ask questions. I acknowledge the pain as each client courageously shares her story. And, at some point, as the end of a first session draws near, I pause and ask gently, "What do *you* want?"

The question is almost always met with silence. It's as if no one has ever asked what *she* wants before. After a few moments of quiet, I hear some version of the following:

- I want to heal.
- I want peace.
- I want to know that I've done my best.

- I want freedom from my anxiety, my addiction, my pain.
- I want to stand up for myself.
- I want to find people who get me.
- I want to fulfill my potential.
- I don't know where to begin.

Most of us want good things—the kinds of things God wants for us. We simply aren't sure how to get what we want. Nobody taught us how.

When faced with the question "What do *you* want?" we hesitate. It's a question that feels foreign, confusing, and even a bit off-putting. *What if I can't get what I want? What if I don't know what I want? What if what I want is selfish?* Instead of looking for clues inside our own hearts, we look for answers everywhere else—other people, experts, friends. Don't get me wrong—all these can be helpful. But what is striking to me is that we ignore the most valuable resource we have; we rarely look to ourselves.

After years of observing this pattern in myself and in others, I began to consider a larger issue: Why is it hard for so many women to recognize—and value—what we think, what we want, and what we need at any given moment? The reason, I discovered, is a hidden issue that is often overlooked.

The Silent Message We've Been Taught

For centuries, most women have been taught to accept a silent message. This message tells us, *Disregard yourself for the sake of others.*

When you disregard someone, you avoid, skip over, or ignore them. You bypass that person as if they are unimportant or insignificant to the situation at hand. Most of us would never disregard someone else in this way, yet we don't even realize the countless ways we've been taught to disregard *ourselves.*[1]

For example, do any of these underlying messages sound familiar to you?

- Sacrifice for others.
- Die to yourself.
- Ignore your emotions.
- You can't trust yourself.

The subtle power of these messages is strong. They exist in the air that we breathe. They are taught throughout homes, schools, and churches. We hear them as impressionable young girls. If you grew up in a religious environment, they were likely even portrayed as biblical.

Instead of growing in understanding yourself, you assume that it's best to focus on other people. You prioritize their needs—and their opinions. And you downplay your negative emotions and your own instincts.

You discount every single thing your mind, your heart, and your body are telling you, because, after all, you were never taught to consider that *you* might hold the key to what's missing.

It doesn't work.

These messages don't lead you to the life God wants for you. In fact, it's a terrible recipe for living. Disregarding your needs, wants, opinions, and desires leads straight to chronic people pleasing, bitterness, and burnout. It leads to loneliness, depression, and unfettered anxiety. And, ultimately, it leads to unhealthy relationships with other people.

It's hard to forge healthy relationships with others if you haven't been taught that what you want and need matters.

It's hard to forge healthy relationships with others if you haven't been taught that what you want and need matters. In contrast, what if you were taught that the key to healthy relationships is learning to honor yourself?

For example, imagine if you had been taught the following:

- Sacrificing for others does not mean betraying yourself.
- Dying to yourself might mean dying to your desire to please someone else.
- Emotions are powerful guides you can harness.
- Trusting yourself is necessary to trust other people.

There has to be a way forward when you find yourself stuck in challenging relationships and situations—a way to love others, set limits when needed, *and* consider yourself.

The good news is, there is.

It's what I call bringing out the best of you.

A Brave New Direction

When you focus on everyone around you, notice what happens: you lose contact with your own sense of self. Your voice gets lost in the chorus of voices around you.

Here's the issue with that method: God has designed your heart, mind, and body with all sorts of incredible ways to discern what's best for your life. But most of us focus all our attention *away* from developing the inner resources we've been given to tackle the problems we face.

What if you were to turn your attention away from all the voices around you for a moment and, instead, turn toward the clearest, calmest version of *yourself*?

To illustrate what I mean, let me tell you a story.

Imagine a young girl in middle school. The big spring dance is approaching. Everybody around her is buzzing about it. Inside, she feels dread. Her friends assume she is as excited as they are. But she has no interest in the drama of waiting for some boy to ask her to dance. She feels stuck between what's expected of her and what she really wants.

Signs are posted all over school. Hallways bustle with kids discussing their plans. All the while, she ponders the possibility of suddenly coming down with the flu for the weekend.

A thought occurs to her: *What if I simply stayed home?* The thought is striking, but could she actually pull that off? What would she tell everyone?

She floats the idea to a few people. Her parents tell her not to be silly—she can't miss the big dance! Her friends tell her she *has* to go. *Everyone* is. She falters, questioning herself: *Maybe they're right. I guess I'll do as they say.*

Now imagine a wise person comes alongside her. It might be a parent, a teacher, or a good friend. Instead of assuming *they* know what's best, what if they helped her answer these questions?

- What is it you want?
- Are you dreading it because you're scared? Or are you dreading it because it doesn't sound fun to you?
- How would you like to spend your time if you do not attend?
- What alternative feels better to you?

As she gets to the root of what *she* wants, the truth begins to surface: "I don't want to go to the dance this year. But I do want to feel included in the lives of my friends." With newfound confidence she steps into action. She tells her friends she can't make the dance on Friday, but she'd love to meet up to hear all about it on Saturday.

Instead of pleasing everyone—and no one—she's made the brave choice to honor herself. Imagine the confidence this girl will have as she moves into her future.

While a middle school dance might seem inconsequential, this decision to honor herself is not. It teaches her that she can discern what she actually wants, and that she has the option to act on it. She will also discover what kind of friends she has. Will they respect her decision? Or will they make fun of her? If they make fun of her, she will face another important decision: Will she back down, or will she stick to her convictions?

Here is the key point: this one seemingly tiny decision has a gigantic ripple effect. Each subsequent choice to honor herself paves a path toward a strong sense of self. On the other hand, if this young woman doesn't learn how to name and honor what she wants, she will head down a path, as so many have, of disregarding herself—a path toward self-betrayal.

The truth is, most of us didn't have a clear choice back then. Most of us were nudged, or shoved, right down that path of disregarding ourselves. But the good news is this: it's never too late to start choosing yourself.

I'm talking about you.

I see you there staring at the problems in your life.

I see you assessing all the opinions and expectations around you.

Would you tune out all the noise and confusion out there just for a moment and tune in to your own heart instead?

What do you notice?

What does it feel like to turn toward *yourself* for a moment?

Take a deep breath and linger right there.

What's it like to consider that *you* might hold the key to new possibilities?

I've been through this. I know it can be hard. But please trust me when I say, when you focus only on the voices out there, you miss out on this key question: *What do I want in here?*

The first step to getting the life that you want is to spend more time developing your own sense of self.

Selfhood Versus Selfishness

Whenever I talk to women about the importance of getting to the root of who they are and what they want, I get pushback like this:

- "But . . . isn't that selfish?"
- "Didn't Jesus teach us to deny ourselves?"
- "Isn't it good to be selfless?"

My answer is this: there is a big difference between selfhood and selfishness. Furthermore, being selfless is not always the right choice. Here is one way to illustrate the differences:

SELFISHNESS	SELFHOOD	SELFLESSNESS
It's all about me.	It's about you and me.	It's all about you.

Selfhood is a psychological term that refers to your individual identity—your "you-ness," as I like to say to my clients. It's what makes you a distinct person from everyone around you.

A strong sense of self is marked by healthy confidence—what I define as a thoughtful awareness of your strengths, preferences, values, and limitations. Uncovering a deep sense of self doesn't just "happen." And it's anything but superficial. In fact, a healthy sense of self is something you develop over time, with care and intention. Selfhood starts by facing yourself honestly. It includes acknowledging what's hard and celebrating the gifts you've been given.

Selfhood is what you bring into your relationships. It gives you the courage to show up bravely, with integrity, even when it means pointing out hard things or honoring your limits. It's an understanding that in any relationship, two people have perspectives that matter, and you are one of those people. In fact, developing a sense of self is the most foundational step to setting healthy boundaries with other people.[2] Yet this step is rarely talked about.

Take a look at the chart below and notice which column resonates with your way of operating. I'll be honest with you—for a long time my thoughts were very much like the ones in the right column.

SELFISHNESS	SELFHOOD	SELFLESSNESS
My wants and needs always come first.	Expressing what I want and need helps me forge healthy relationships with others.	My wants and needs don't matter.
I pursue what I want—no matter who gets hurt.	I develop my own talents *and* help others develop theirs.	I bury my talents—even though it hurts me.
I always advocate for my needs. I never defer to others.	I consider my needs *and* the needs of others.	I never state my needs. I always defer to others.
First and foremost, I ask, "What's in it for me?"	I give to others *and* I know how to receive.	I work hard for others. I don't know how to receive.

Selfhood is necessary to establish healthy relationships, live out your potential, and create the life you desire. It's not being selfish, and it's also not being a doormat.

Without selfhood, your decisions are driven by guilt and fear. You take the path of least resistance or work overtime to please everyone else. You prioritize the opinions of other people instead of honoring your own authentic wants and needs.

You don't show up as the best of who you are.

You don't live out of the best of who God created you to be.

being taught to develop his strength. In order to love and lead others, you have to develop a strong sense of self.

In order to show up in relationships as God intended, you have to become who you are. You have to become your true self.

Your true self is the person you really are, the person God made. It involves a deep understanding of your strengths, needs, values, and purpose. It's finding—and expressing—your voice with other people. It's knowing that you have what it takes to course-correct, even when you make mistakes.

Becoming your true self is a process of learning to say yes to what matters most:

- Yes to your convictions
- Yes to your health
- Yes to your sanity
- Yes to asking for help
- Yes to healthy boundaries
- Yes to your talents

And the best part is, as you become your true self, you discover that you have more goodness, more wisdom, and more capacity to bring to the people around you.

The Best of You

I wrote *The Best of You* to share proven steps any woman can take to turn the pain of feeling stuck into the empowerment of discovering—and becoming—your true self in God.

In the pages to come, I will walk you through a process of carefully taking inventory of your life—including all that's been hard—in anticipation of the best that's yet to come. Here's my promise to you:

- You'll learn to get to the root of what you actually need and desire.
- You'll learn how to identify—and work your way through—the painful patterns that keep you stuck.
- You'll learn to grieve and release what can't be and turn toward new possibilities.
- You'll learn to turn away from past harm and take charge of your future.
- You'll learn to envision—and create—the life and relationships you want with God's help.

I've been on this journey myself and I've helped hundreds of women discover this new way to live. When you focus on the work of becoming your true self, you start creating the life and relationships you desire. You start anchoring yourself in the answer to this crucial question: What do *you* want?[8]

Together, in the pages ahead, we're going to answer these life-changing questions:

- What new direction do *you* want to take?
- What or who do *you* want more of in your life?
- What needs are *you* dying to have met?
- What convictions are *you* aching to protect?
- What step can *you* take toward unlocking your potential?
- What brings out the best of *you*?

Don't feel surprised if a part of you feels skeptical—or even fearful—about this approach. That's a normal response if no one has ever taught you how to prioritize your own needs and desires. It's possible you've never considered these questions on a deep level before.

But I can guarantee that staying stuck in fear and uncertainty is no way to live. Discovering what brings out the best of you, on the other hand, opens a whole new range of possibilities.

When you get to the root of your wants, needs, values, and even your limitations, you develop newfound courage, confidence, and clarity. These qualities are good for you and good for your loved ones.

Are you willing to consider a new way to view yourself as a woman—a gold mine of wisdom, possibility, and purpose?

Will you join me on a journey of discovering the best of you?

Reflections

1. What is a challenging relationship or situation that you are currently facing?
2. Regarding this situation, consider the question, "What do you want?"
3. Notice what comes to mind. As an action step, consider the following exercise.
   - Make a list of eight to ten statements, each one starting with "I want."
   - Don't censor yourself.
   - Don't be surprised if the statements are contradictory.
   - Don't worry if any of the statements feel selfish or selfless. Simply notice and write it down.
   - Invite God to join you in this process of observing what you wrote.

Chapter 2

How Did I Get Here?

The Cocktail of Codependency

ANGIE FLASHED A BIG SMILE AS SHE SPED INTO MY OFFICE, dressed as if she'd just been to the gym. Setting her gigantic water bottle next to her, she perched on the couch's edge, her body taut.

"Thanks so much for meeting with me. I know how busy you are!" she said, her speech rapid, as if she didn't want to take any more of my time than was necessary.

She explained to me that she ran a well-respected nonprofit that supported local foster children, hosted get-togethers for friends, and spent much of her free time helping others. But, inside, she was feeling hopeless and distressed.

"I'm depressed," she said without showing any outward sign of it. Her appearance made her seem like the picture of efficiency and competence. Eyes wide, she sat up straight on the couch, ready to bolt like a young colt the minute the clock told her our time was up.

"It makes me so mad. I try everything—working out, eating healthy, praying. But no matter what I do, the truth is, I'm having a hard time getting out of bed."

Angie had been diagnosed with depression years prior and was on antidepressant medication. It helped a little bit, but for the most part she continued to feel empty inside.

Here was a woman who was doing everything "right." She was tending to her physical health and had sought a doctor to help stabilize her mental health. She prayed regularly and helped other people. She was literally caring for hundreds of orphans, for goodness' sake. Yet some part of her remained deeply wounded and downcast. She couldn't access any real sense of joy or wonder. She struggled to experience God's love, even though she believed factually that it was real.

Angie knew how to work hard and care for others. She knew how to pray and seek God's guidance. But inside she remained depressed and disconnected.

Spiritually Strong, Emotionally Struggling

Every week in my work, I witness this inner tension. It happens to married women and those who are single, to moms, executives, and ministry leaders. All kinds of women are spiritually strong but emotionally struggling.

If trusting in God was the cure, they would have been fixed. Yet here they are, sitting in my office, wondering, *How did I get here?*

They're overwhelmed, anxious, and running on empty. They feel like they're doing everything they've been taught to do. They're working hard, trying to be kind, even learning to care for themselves and set boundaries.

Yet, they're torn up on the inside.

They believed God would help them, and still do. But each of them has bumped up against a painful reality: you can trust God and still feel anxious, lonely, overwhelmed, and broken inside.

You can be strong spiritually and remain stuck emotionally at the exact place where you got hurt in the past. You can have confidence in God and be completely ill-equipped for the land mines life will inevitably present. You can treat others well, as you've been taught, only to discover that people will take advantage of you.

You can trust God and still feel anxious, lonely, overwhelmed, and broken inside.

Why does this happen?

After decades of integrating faith and psychology, I believe there are three realities of life that lead to women feeling stuck and disempowered.

1. Childhood wounds
2. Confusing church messages
3. Cultural conditioning

Taken together, these ingredients create what I call a "cocktail of codependency," a cocktail that is insidiously harming millions of women.

Codependency is a pattern of relating in which you focus so much on other people, you become disconnected from your true self.[1] Typically someone with codependent tendencies isn't aware of this disconnect. They've simply learned to cope with their own pain by focusing on someone else's. It's a form of self-betrayal that keeps you from the healthy two-way relationships God designed you to have—including with God. For centuries, spiritual leaders have observed that it is impossible to draw close to God when you are distant from your own self.[2] And the same truth applies to your relationships with other people. When you are disconnected from your true self, you are disconnected from other people. Yet codependency is a relationship pattern that exists in epidemic proportions.

Let's start unpacking this problem by exploring the first ingredient, childhood wounds, often referred to as trauma.

What Is Trauma?

When you hear the word *trauma*, you might assume that it only applies to extreme situations. But when understood correctly, trauma is a reality that touches more people than you might think. *Trauma* is the word psychologists use to describe the impact of a painful, frightening, or overwhelming event.[3] Specifically, the impact of a traumatic event exceeds your capacity to cope with or process what happened in a constructive way. If left unattended, a wound is created that doesn't get healed.[4]

Prior to the last few decades, trauma was understood primarily in the context of a terrible one-time event. For example, soldiers who returned from war experienced symptoms of trauma, including flashbacks, anxiety, and night terrors. Other horrific experiences, such as being raped, witnessing a murder, or a near-death experience were—and still are—also considered traumatic.

But psychologists began to realize that trauma was a much bigger player in people's lives than originally thought. They started to realize that trauma comes in a variety of shapes and sizes—some big "T" trauma and some little "t" trauma—but all creating an impact. In particular, they started to realize the effects of relational trauma.

Examples of relational trauma include

- Physical abuse
- Emotional neglect
- Sexual abuse
- Verbal abuse
- Constant manipulation or criticism
- Witnessing arguing or violence between family members

- Bullying
- Ostracism by peers
- Various forms of racism[5]
- Uncovering a betrayal, such as infidelity
- Perceived failures at school, work, or in relationships
- A sudden or unexplained loss

The list could go on, but the key point to remember is that clinicians no longer think of trauma as the result of a rare, one-time event. In fact, psychiatrist Bessel van der Kolk noted that "the consequences of caretaker abuse and neglect are vastly more common and complex than the impact of hurricanes or motor vehicle accidents."[6]

Instead, trauma more simply defined is an *unwitnessed pain*. Painful events bring on a cascade of complex emotions such as fear, shock, anger, and a sense of vulnerability. Stress chemicals, like cortisol, are released, affecting the brain, body, and responses to other people. If the pain isn't acknowledged and healed through loving connection, a wound is created that can fester for years.

Children are particularly vulnerable to the impact of trauma because they don't have the capacity to process complex, emotionally charged situations. When left alone with any sort of pain, children will infuse events with meaning that is often self-shaming. As Dr. Gabor Maté said in his powerful film *The Wisdom of Trauma*, "Children don't get traumatized because they are hurt. Children are traumatized because they are alone with the hurt."[7] While our souls are designed to heal from painful events, they are not designed to heal in isolation from other people. *God didn't design you to be alone in your pain.*

For example, maybe you were raised in a home where your parents fought constantly. If no one helped you understand what was happening, you may have told yourself the fighting was your fault, even though their arguments had nothing to do with you. Or maybe you were raised by a parent who was self-absorbed or absent from you emotionally. You may have told yourself that you were not worth being loved or cherished.

As you grow older, you absorb these faulty messages deep down inside, outside of your conscious awareness. You carry them into your adult relationships. These messages linger, and they play a key role in what shows up as anxiety, depression, and unsatisfying relationships later in life. In fact, some form of trauma—whether big "T" or little "t"—lurks in the background of almost every human being who lives on this planet. It's impossible to live in this world and not pick up a wound or two.

When I was first studying to be a counselor, trauma was barely discussed. Instead, the focus back then was on the idea of "mental illness." If you struggled with anxiety, you had an "anxiety disorder." Or, if you struggled with depression, you had a "depressive disorder." It was almost as if you could "catch" these disorders, as one might catch the flu or some other illness. According to this way of looking at mental health, the roots of interpersonal problems were not necessarily considered. You looked at symptoms, created a diagnosis, and treated the person accordingly, often with medicine or some version of talk therapy. This is what my client Angie had experienced prior to coming to see me for help that day.

Over time, however, therapists started to note the disparity between the mental illness model and what we actually encountered with real live people in therapy.

I was one of the therapists noticing this disparity. As a new counselor, working at a college counseling center, I grew frustrated and angry with what I saw as a very limiting approach. Here were some of the issues I confronted:

- Why would I diagnose a young man with a mental "illness" when what he's really struggling with is the fact that his stepmother abused him? Of course he's depressed. The pain of that abuse has been living silently inside of him.

- It doesn't make sense to put this young girl on medication against her own wishes. Her anxiety seems warranted. Her parents have abandoned her, leaving her completely on her own, without a support system. Of course she is anxious!

Little did I know, as I was fuming against my psychology training, that experts had been researching the far-reaching impact of relational trauma for years. In 2014, Dr. Van der Kolk published what would become his trailblazing *New York Times* bestselling book *The Body Keeps the Score*, in which he details the prevalence of interpersonal trauma and how it affects the brain and nervous system. He would argue, much as I had intuited, that we do hurting people no favors by telling them they are mentally ill when their bodies are simply responding to painful or toxic circumstances in ways that are necessary for survival. In fact, one might argue that when someone is acting out as a result of unhealed wounds, their body is working properly.

As the research has grown, we now understand that much of what we used to assume was mental illness is actually an indicator of trauma.[8] Clinicians are increasingly looking at anxiety, depression, and other emotional problems not as illnesses to diagnose but as cues to start asking these key questions:

- What happened?[9]
- What faulty messages did you pick up?
- What unhealed wounds are still lodged in your body?

Left untended, these wounds can impede your ability to live from a calm, centered place internally. Instead, you operate out of survival mode.

Your Inner Alert System

God designed you with a sophisticated, state-of-the-art system to alert you to danger in your environment. It's your nervous system, which affects your emotions, perceptions, and nearly every decision you make. This inner alert system helps you keep yourself safe emotionally and physically.[10]

The problem is that unhealed wounds from your past affect this system, influencing how you react to situations in your present. These reactions are embedded in your body and operate outside your conscious control. Without realizing it, your brain automatically jumps to conclusions about a present situation based on past conditioning.

THE FOUR FEAR RESPONSES:

1. **Fight:** attack, confront
2. **Flight:** flee, avoid
3. **Freeze:** numb, isolate
4. **Fawn:** please, win over

In the face of real threats, these survival responses are constructive. But trauma can cause your body to misread a threat. For example, it can cause you to react to *minor* threats—or even instances of healthy vulnerability—as if they were a *major* attack on your safety. Trauma can also cause you to *under*react to actual threats. Your body can grow accustomed to a heightened state of arousal and stress. As a result, you might be drawn to the familiarity of stressful relationships.

You might already be familiar with the idea of a "fight, flight, or freeze" response. When you sense danger, your inner alert system kicks into high gear. Your heart rate quickens, your palms grow sweaty, and your body grows tense as it prepares to protect itself.[11] If you tend toward "fight," you might get louder, physically act out, or run headfirst into a conflict. If you tend toward "flight," you might run away, hide, or simply avoid any semblance of confrontation. If you "freeze," you might find yourself shutting down altogether. You might disconnect from emotional cues as a way to tolerate the pain. This is what psychologists call *disassociation*.

Think about your own relationships: Do you run headlong into conflict (fight)? Or do you move away from it as fast as you can (flight)? Do you sometimes find yourself checking out mentally or emotionally altogether (freeze)? Now, think back to when you were young. Do you remember when, where, or why you started to adopt that tendency?

The important thing to know is that these impulses are conditioned responses. Something happened outside of you that stirred up stress or fear inside of you. So your body figured out how to respond to protect itself. Over time, that response became reflexive. That means your body learned to respond to certain cues in the environment— without you even having a chance to think about it.

Here's an example. As a young girl, maybe your mother criticized you constantly. At the time you didn't know that what she was doing was cruel. After all, she was your mom, the only one you ever knew. But that criticism stirred up something negative inside you. It didn't feel good. Your nervous system got activated and became poised to protect you. Maybe you chose to avoid your mom or hide from her jabs. Or maybe you fought back, learning how to land your own punches.

At some point, you received a reward or positive outcome for whichever path you chose. If you fought, you found that you could gain power. Sure, it wasn't pleasant to argue with your mom, but at least you felt a rush of adrenaline as a result of standing up for yourself. If you fled, you found that you could avoid most of the pain. Sure, you sacrificed closeness with your mom, but at least you weren't getting criticized.

All the while, your body was being conditioned by that behavior. As an adult, however, that conditioned response may no longer be appropriate for certain problems that surface. Maybe your partner, who is genuinely trying to be helpful says, "Hey, your shirt is on inside out."

He's kind, not critical, just looking out for you. But his words activate the same feelings your mom's did in the past. Your body goes into fight mode, and suddenly you're on the attack: "Stop criticizing me!" Your spouse, who wasn't in fact criticizing you, is confused and dumbfounded.

Your body took over and misread the cues. Maybe you even know that you overreacted, prompting shame and embarrassment. But you can't figure out how to stop this reaction to anyone who seems remotely critical.

Here's the good news: you can learn to identify the warning signs that your body is moving into a fight, flight, or freeze response. You can notice what is happening inside your body *before* you act out. You can increase the time between when your conditioned instinct kicks in and when you react, giving you an opportunity to *choose your response*. We'll get into how to do that in upcoming chapters.

But first, let's look at a fourth survival response, one that is often mistakenly reinforced as positive, especially in women.

The Fawn Response

As a young child, I grew up in the wild mountains of Wyoming. We bumped into all kinds of wildlife, but there is nothing like bumping into a baby fawn, laying in the grass all curled up and cuddly. They don't run, grunt, or show fear when you find them the way other wild animals do. Instead, they make themselves small so you can barely see them. By becoming small and appearing "safe," they attempt to keep themselves from harm. (Who wants to hurt a baby fawn?)

It's an extremely adaptive survival response. Indeed, as psychologists studied the impact of childhood wounding on adult behavior, they detected an additional conditioned response, known as the "fawn" response.[12] The fawn response doesn't look like fight, flight, or freeze. Instead, fawning looks like being nice. It can be challenging to recognize, but it's the response I see most often in my work with women.

To illustrate, let's return to Angie's story for a moment.

Angie had grown up in a highly conflicted home. Her dad would scream at her mom for hours (fight). Her mom would cry, plead, then flee to the bedroom (flight). All the while, Angie watched, fearful and wide-eyed. The fighting left her feeling terribly anxious and alone. But, as a young child, she had no idea what that uncomfortable feeling in her stomach was. She only knew that she wanted to feel better.

She remembered one particular fight vividly. It was awful. As she peeked out from behind the staircase, she couldn't bear to tear her eyes away from the violent clash. Watching is what kept her connected to her parents, whose love she desperately needed. She wanted to scream at them to stop, but she knew that if she entered into the conflict, they'd only turn their anger on her.

Desperate to soothe the searing pain in her belly, Angie made herself as small and unthreatening as possible. When the fighting died down, she tiptoed into the kitchen, cleaned up the mess they'd made, and started dinner. Later, when her parents returned, no one said a word about the fight. But her mom said, "You're such a good girl, Angie."

In that moment, Angie learned a powerful message. She learned that when she felt anxious, she could get a hit of relief if she would only shrink herself down, camouflage her own pain, and make *someone else* feel good.

Unbeknownst to her, Angie had been conditioned to *fawn*.

In the face of her arguing parents, she became small, tiny, "safe." If she could be helpful enough, calming enough, and pleasing enough, her mom would feel better and her dad would de-escalate. If she pretended that her own needs weren't important—and took care of others—then she could feel better. Without realizing it, Angie's parents had conditioned her to betray her own little self to get the love and attention she craved.

Like Angie, I also learned to fawn. Even though the circumstances were less extreme, an unhealed wound inside me developed into a painful pattern of disconnecting from my own self to please other people.

The Armor of Invisibility

As a young girl, I learned to play it safe by staying invisible. It didn't start out that way. It started out with a sixth-grade production of *Alice in Wonderland*. Some part of me longed to play the brash, over-the-top Queen of Hearts. I couldn't believe it when I got the part.

My mom and I spent months preparing and sewing the red dress, complete with the black and yellow checkered panel down the front and a stiff white collar that would stand up like it did in the movie. We even bought bright red Lee Press-On Nails, so I could point the Queen's villainous fingers with authority. On opening night, I was dressed and ready. I knew my lines and my costume was perfect.

But when it came time to take the stage and actually play the part, something inside me crumbled. Terrified, I suddenly thought, *Who am I to think I can be this person?*

Then I started to look around at everybody else.

I watched as my friend Gretchen, playing Alice, sauntered across the stage, masterfully singing her lines. My other friend Brandi embodied the charming and funny Dodo Bird, just as she carried herself in real life.

Doubt flooded my brain: *They're so much better than me. I can't play this part. Gretchen could do it—she's so good at everything. Brandi is so easy-going. See how she's making everyone laugh!*

As I looked at every girl around me, all my internal angst could be summarized in one sentence: *I should be more like that other girl.*

I completely lost sight of my own self. Worse, in the midst of all of my mental gymnastics, I forgot to play my own part. I missed the cue to say my first lines, and when I did, they were awkward and fumbling.

After my scene, I rushed offstage, humiliated, ripping off the fake fingernails underneath my cloak. *Who did I think I was, trying to play this bold, brash character?* I fled home, ashamed and embarrassed. But nobody knew how I felt. I didn't tell anybody.

Instead, I praised my friends and told them how great *they* were. I made fun of myself and told self-deprecating stories. I pretended that I didn't care. And I continued to self-deprecate for the next few decades.

To this day I still remember that painful moment onstage. And I have learned that there's a reason we remember. At an incredibly formative age, I took up a belief that would follow me all the way into adulthood: *Don't put yourself out there. Don't take up space.* I learned to stay as small and invisible as possible. By doing so, I'd never have to feel the kind of shame I had experienced that night. I shoved aside my dreams and focused on making other people feel good. Without realizing it, I inhabited a pattern of relating to others that would eventually lead to chronic loneliness, exhaustion, and burnout.

I told myself this was "being kind." I told myself I was "humble." I even told myself it was "sacrificial." Make no mistake, though—this wasn't primarily about helping others. It was about protecting me. It was my way of creating armor to avoid being vulnerable. I call it the "armor of invisibility."

Not surprisingly, I was praised for these behaviors, and that praise felt good.

"You're so giving," my teachers would tell me.

"You're so easy to have around," my friends would say.

Fawning became a way to earn love.

It kept me safe. Just like that fawn in the wilderness, I could stay small and blend into my surroundings. I could make myself as unthreatening as possible to avoid the dangers of feeling like a fool or being too much. But it was also incredibly damaging to my core sense of self. It was as if I was wearing a thick invisibility cloak, and it would be decades before I'd learn how to take that cloak off.

What I needed was to learn how to assert myself, face my fears, and step into the light as my true self. I needed to discover and nurture what brought out the best of me. Unfortunately, I learned the opposite lessons in the places I turned to for instruction.

When Church Messages Reinforce a Fawn Response

As I entered adulthood, I found that fawning was affirmed within many contexts, including faith communities. I have also found that to be the case for most of the women I counsel.

In fact, fawning is often revered.

Think about it: you're a woman who has been hiding for years, playing small, trying to keep yourself safe by making everyone around you happy. Parts of you may yearn for more. You might even feel a little angry. You start noticing a growing murmuring inside:

- *Wait, is it* my *job to make sure everyone else is okay?*
- *What about what* I *need?*
- *Do* I *get a say?*

But your faith community doubles down on messages encouraging you to focus on others and deny your true feelings. In fact, some church messages encourage a damaging practice that psychologists call *spiritual bypassing*. Spiritual bypassing is a way of using religious platitudes to encourage people to avoid dealing honestly with wounds and painful emotions like anger, grief, loneliness, or fear.

Here are some examples of spiritual bypassing:

- "Anger is bad. Pray it away."
- "God would never let you feel lonely."
- "If you had more faith, you wouldn't feel that way."
- "Starve your fear. It's the enemy of your faith!"
- *"Choose joy"* (said with fists clenched).

Instead of providing the healing balm of compassion and loving presence, these messages minimize, over-spiritualize, and encourage you to stay hidden. In effect, it's wounding the already wounded in the name of faith. It's saying, if you want to *appear* faithful, keep your pain to yourself.

These messages reinforce what has already been deeply conditioned inside you:

- Your feelings don't matter.
- It's better to stay small.
- Just stay focused on others.
- Don't be a bother.

Instead of seeking to understand your emotions or your areas of wounding, you are encouraged to ask God to get rid of them. Instead of letting your pain or anger lead you to assertiveness or healthier boundaries with others, you hide these emotions in the name of being selfless. Instead of getting the healing you need, you bury your pain even deeper, shaming yourself for the struggles you face.

Spiritual bypassing is not what the Bible teaches.[13] Jesus welcomed the beat-up, downtrodden, hopeless, even doubting souls he encountered. He didn't shame them or shove them aside.

A church family is an important place to grow, give and receive care, and learn about God's love. But, like a family with misguided or abusive parents, when church messages encourage you to disconnect from your God-given self, it's incredibly damaging.

You can't heal what you don't acknowledge. You can't transform what you've pretended doesn't exist. You don't heal in the context of shame, criticism, or spiritual bypassing. You heal—and become your true self in God—in the context of safety, honesty, love, and compassion.

But if you weren't taught these ways by your church or your parents, how would you know any better? How would you discover the healing God wants for you? Before we get there, let's take a look at another factor that adds to the problem: cultural conditioning.

The Cultural Conditioning of Women

As women, we deal with a third ingredient within the cocktail of codependency that can contribute to unhealthy patterns of relating. In addition to childhood wounds and confusing church messages, we live in a culture that has historically conditioned women to please, shrink, and hide their voices.[14] These messages may be changing, but they continue to linger. In fact, many of our mothers and grandmothers grew up in generations of women who faced extremely limited options.

For example, some of our great-grandmothers weren't allowed to vote, and many of our mothers and grandmothers weren't allowed to apply for their own credit cards or run a marathon! Imagine growing up with these pervasive cultural messages:

- Your voice doesn't count.
- You can't depend on yourself.
- Your talents don't matter.
- Your body isn't worthy of respect.[15]

If you don't think these messages still affect women today, consider that women are diagnosed with depression and anxiety at significantly higher rates than men.[16] Let me be clear: this statistic does not show that there is something wrong with women. This statistic reveals the lingering legacy of *misunderstanding* and devaluing women. Women are tough. We're in the trenches mending the fabric of our society. We're nurturing children, supporting our friends, strengthening our communities, and producing important work alongside our colleagues.

Yet, we've also paid a price.

The problem is this: women are taught to put others first before they are taught to cherish themselves.

Millions of women have been told that it's more important to lay down their lives,[17] rather than the equally important truth that their lives are precious and theirs to protect.[18]

> **Women are taught to put others first before they are taught to cherish themselves.**

Most women have been taught to die to a life that they haven't yet learned how to live. Instead of encouraging women to stay small and sacrifice for others, it's time to encourage a counterbalancing message.

Come Alive to Yourself

When Jesus walked the earth, he spent time with different kinds of people, and he had different messages for each of them. Jesus' teachings are not one-size-fits-all.

In particular, notice how Jesus treated women.

- Jesus stood up for women (John 8:1–11; Luke 7:36–50).
- Jesus confided in women (John 4:21–28).
- Jesus did not shame women (Matthew 26:6–13).
- Jesus empowered women (Luke 10:38–42; Luke 8:42–48).
- Jesus gave women a voice (Matthew 28:1–10; Luke 8:1–3).

Jesus lifted up those who cried out for help, even when their communities despised them. In contrast, Jesus leveled his harshest criticism toward powerful leaders who pushed aside women, the suffering, and the marginalized.

With these principles in mind, what did Jesus mean when he said to "deny yourself" in order to follow him?[19] Let's take a look at what that phrase really means.

Jesus used a metaphor of a grain of wheat to describe the process of dying to yourself:

"Listen carefully: Unless a grain of wheat is buried in the ground, dead to the world, it is never any more than a grain of wheat. But if it is buried, it sprouts and reproduces itself many times over. In the same way, anyone who holds on to life just as it is destroys that life. But if you let it go, reckless in your love, you'll have it forever, real and eternal."[20]

Consider this. The grain of wheat represents your old ways of surviving—the fighting, fleeing, and fawning; the pleasing, performing, and hiding. Those ways worked for a time, but they no longer serve you, or anyone. You have to change. You have to "die" to old ways.

It's hard. It might even feel like a loss initially. After all, these ways served you in the past. But to become a truer version of yourself, you have to release these old ways. It's the only way to grow.

Dying to yourself means letting go of old ways you've learned to please or perform for others, of ways you learned to hide. It means coming alive to the person you really are, the person God made. This idea is echoed in other Bible passages. Here's what the apostle John said:

But whoever did want him, who believed he was who he claimed and would do what he said, *he made to be their true selves, their child-of-God selves.*[21]

When you follow Jesus, you become even more of your true self, your child-of-God self, the beautiful soul God made. We know from Jesus' words that the process can feel like death, like you are losing all that you have known. Indeed, letting go of old ways can be painful.

Change is no small thing. But here's the promise: you are dying to old ways in order to become the brave, light-bearing woman God made.

This process is not a rigid form of self-denial. It's not a "grin and bear it" way of surviving in the world. If you're taking that approach, I'll be honest: part of you is hanging on to old ways.

Instead, consider this. What if dying to yourself means dying to these destructive tendencies?

- Toxic patterns of relating to other people
- Pleasing someone as a way to get love
- Shame and self-hatred
- Burying painful emotions, like sadness, loneliness, or anger
- Perfecting yourself to earn approval
- Playing small so others won't be threatened by you
- Believing that you don't matter and that your life does not have value

What if dying to yourself means dying to the lie that God does not have more for you?

What if dying to yourself means dying to the lie that you don't have what it takes?

What if dying to yourself means coming alive to what brings out the best of you?

This is what I believe it means to grow in emotional and spiritual health. It means dying to toxic ways of relating to God, yourself, and other people. It means identifying who or what brings out the worst of you—and taking steps to change those patterns. And, most importantly, it means saying yes to the Good Shepherd as he leads you on this journey of becoming your truest self.

This work isn't magic. It takes care, courage, and persistence. But, as you learn how to observe old ways of being and take brave steps toward healing, you'll soon find that you have exactly what it takes.

Reflections

1. Consider a challenging relationship or situation. It might be the same one you identified at the end of chapter 1.
2. What are "old ways" you have picked up related to that situation as a result of childhood wounds, church messages, or cultural conditioning? For example:
   - It's better to stay small.
   - I shouldn't feel angry or sad.
   - My voice doesn't count.
3. What is a new message God might be inviting you to consider instead?

Chapter 3

How Do I Find My Way Out?

Observing Painful Patterns

IF YOU ARE A WOMAN WHO LEARNED TO HIDE OR MAKE yourself small, please know this is not the life God has for you. If you are a woman who has felt like you have to mute your personality, your take-charge attitude, or your leadership abilities, please know this is not the life God has for you.

God wants the best of you.

And God wants the best *for* you.

God wants for you to heal, for you to come out from hiding.

God wants for you to learn how to grow big inside yourself, full of his Spirit and might.

God wants for you to learn how to stand up for the convictions inside of you.[1]

But I have found through my work as a counselor that many women are slowly giving up on these truths. Don't get me wrong: most women are not giving up on being helpful or kind to others. Most women are not giving up on God. But after working with women for over two decades, the truth is that many are slowly and subtly giving up on parts of themselves that need healing.

In fact, this is exactly where I found myself well into my thirties. I loved God and sought to care for other people. But I had almost given up on the idea that maybe, just maybe, God wanted me to bring out the best of *me*.

The Hidden You

It started with an "almost" breakup.

"I love you, but I don't think we're ready to get married," the man I was dating said one night as we sipped drinks at a local restaurant. I was stunned. At the age of thirty-seven, I had never been married. We had dated for more than a year, and I was ready for him to put a ring on it.

Joe was a widower with two young children when we met. He had loved his first wife, the mother of his kids, and had cared for her and for them through her debilitating illness as she passed away. Based on what he'd been through in life and the way God made him, he wasn't someone who shied away from hard conversations.

"I'm committed to you. I'm not leaving. Please hear me say that. But we have work to do," Joe said. "I love your mind and your heart. But I can't get to the root of who you are and what you want out of your life. Sometimes it feels like you're hiding from me. If we can't both put all our cards on the table—the good and what's hard—it won't be healthy for either of us."

As he spoke these words, the life force sucked out of me. I felt as if I'd left my body and was floating above the table, where I watched myself nodding and listening attentively, somehow willing myself to move a water glass over to my mouth. Shame had washed over me, and while I was aware of a terrible feeling, I was simultaneously aware of myself staying calm and present with him.

I was witnessing my own fawn response in action.

As an adult, I had traded the invisibility cloak of my teen years for the expert position of full-time helper, otherwise known as a psychologist. I had honed my ability to focus on other people. No longer just a helpful daughter or an encouraging friend, I was now a bona fide doctor of healing. I made my living tending to other people's problems, and I was good at it—so good that I could lose myself in it.

I worked for God now. I was his helper. I didn't need other people.

I was proud of the way that I helped others. But part of me longed to be seen. I hadn't yet learned to let God's healing light shine onto the inside of me, let alone let someone else into my longings, fears, and vulnerabilities.

Hearing these words from this man I deeply admired touched on a wound that went all the way back to my childhood, back to that sixth-grade girl buried deep inside who longed to show up big in her own life.

I am not going to leave you.

I love you.

I'm committed to you.

As I sat there listening, still detached from my body, those words somehow reached me.

Wait, he's not leaving me. Then what is he saying?

I love you. But I can't find you.

I could not make sense of this message.

On one hand, it sounded as if he was saying the exact words I feared—he could not *see* me.

On the other hand, he was saying something new, words I had always longed to hear.

I won't leave you. I want to find you.

The shame lingered, but I smiled and nodded through the rest of our dinner.

The next day, the battle within me began.

That jerk! What gives him the right to tell me to work on myself?

Look at all his flaws. They are way worse than mine.

I'm being like Jesus by always focusing on other people. What does he have to say for himself?

Tempted to pick up the phone and download all the terrible things about him to my friends, some part of me wouldn't let me. (Well, maybe I did a little bit.)

"He's not wrong," I wrote in my journal.

Something deep inside me knew that he was right. When you have lived decades of your life camouflaging who you are—even while you're doing "good things for God"—you get that it might be hard for someone else to find you, to know who you really are.

Joe had my attention.

God had my attention.

But here was my dilemma: How in the world do you stop being camouflage when it's all you've ever been? How do you let someone in when you've worked overtime to stay hidden?

I had learned to cope in relationships—and feel like a valuable person—by always focusing on others. Yet God had brought into my path a man who had exactly zero interest in all my efforts to focus on him. To experience the kind of love I actually wanted, I had to learn to make myself visible.

Understandably, part of me experienced Joe's words as a rejection. But he wasn't rejecting me. Instead, he was desperately trying to get a message to the hidden me buried deep within:

- I want *you*.
- I want the real you that is hiding.
- This camouflage keeps me from the person I want to spend my life with.

I knew he was right. He wanted to know all of me—not just the pleasing, helpful perception of me I was so good at creating. And I was the only one who could open that door. Instead of focusing on others, I had to start focusing on the deep, life-changing work of bringing forth the person I really was.

In order to be known by other people, you have to show up as your true self. In order to show up as your true self, you have to face your wounds.

In my case, it was Joe who served as a catalyst for me to dig deeper into the work of facing unhealed wounds and confronting aspects of my conditioning that had encouraged me to hide. But the truth is that God was the driving force behind the healing I would subsequently find.

In order to show up as your true self, you have to face your wounds.

In the same way, God wants to heal and draw out the real you, including the parts of you that have learned to stay hidden. To join God in this effort, you have to start paying attention. You have to become aware of the ways you've been wounded, the methods you've used to cope, and the countless subtle and not-so-subtle messages of your conditioning. This work is tender. It requires compassion, courage, and care. And it requires a strong foundation of trust, the cornerstone of which is developing trust with *yourself.*

After all, how can you trust someone else with the real you if *you* aren't sure what they'll find?

Are You Supposed to Distrust Yourself?

There was a reason I hadn't spent time doing the hard work of uncovering my real self. Like many women, I was taught to distrust myself. I didn't yet know that I could become true to the woman God had made me to be. I didn't yet know that learning to show up as myself in all my strength and all my tenderness was key to forging healthy relationships with other people. And I didn't yet know that learning to trust myself in that process of becoming is the only way to build trusting relationships with other people. Learning to trust yourself is the only way to learn how to trust other people.

Trust is a loaded word we toss around without really understanding what it means. Simply put, trust is the "belief in the reliability, truth, ability, or strength of someone or something."[2] Many of us understand and believe that God is trustworthy. And some of us have been lucky enough to stumble upon trustworthy qualities in other people. But most of us have no clue what it means to trust ourselves. In fact, you might have been taught *not* to trust yourself.

If you grew up in a faith community, you may have been taught to distrust yourself based on a specific Bible verse that says, "The human heart is the most deceitful of all things, and desperately wicked."[3] The problem is that this verse is taken out of context. As my coauthor Kimberly Miller and I detailed in our book *Boundaries for Your Soul*, the very same prophet who declared this bad news about our deceitful state also foretold the good news about what would happen one day when Jesus would come.[4] In fact, Jeremiah prophesied the solution to this problem in the coming of God's Spirit: "I will put my law in their minds and *write it on their hearts*."[5] Through the power of God's Spirit, what had only been available externally (the law) is now available internally (the Spirit).[6]

This teaching in Jeremiah is underscored by an idea in psychology related to *locus of control*. When you have an internal locus of control, you tend to look to resources within yourself—including God's Spirit—to affect change, make decisions, and create impact. You have a sense that you can, to some degree, take charge of your life. In contrast, when you lean toward an *external locus of control*, you tend to view what happens to you as outside of your control. You view external sources, such as circumstances, "fate," or other people, as responsible for your well-being.

An internal locus of control relates to higher levels of confidence and improved mental health, while an external locus of control tends to correlate with increased feelings of anxiety and depression.[7] Some psychologists believe that an internal locus of control is one of the most important factors in healthy coping throughout life.[8] It's not that you don't *also* need trustworthy people and a healthy community around you, but in order to engage those external resources in helpful ways, you have to be able to rely on your inner resources, including emotional and physical cues, critical thinking, and wisdom, to guide your actions. This is why any system that keeps individuals from developing free will and personal agency—whether it's a government, a religious institution, or a family—is so destructive.

Not surprisingly, women are conditioned toward an external locus of control, while men are conditioned toward an internal locus of control.[9] Women are taught to look outside of themselves for solutions. And, I would argue, this is particularly true in faith communities. But focusing only on external resources isn't healthy. In fact, research in the psychology of religion has shown that when you recognize that God is empowering *you* to take action, it's good for your mental *and* spiritual health.[10] It's also what we see taught in Scripture.[11]

Part of trusting God means *actively participating* in the work of developing trust in the capability and strengths God has given you. Trusting yourself is believing in your own capacity to be reliable, true, capable, discerning, and strong. You build trust with yourself as you

- face areas of wounding honestly, with compassion;
- become aware of your needs and how to meet them;
- recognize and respond to cues from your emotions and body;
- notice and heed red flags in relationships; and
- identify and honor your values, intuition, and convictions.

To be clear, trusting yourself is *not*

- "you doing you" regardless of the cost,
- acting out of emotions recklessly,
- ignoring your own blind spots,
- never seeking help or advice, or
- assuming you're always right.

As humans, we are not ultimately trustworthy like God is. We fail all the time. But we also have access to the Spirit of God inside the beautiful soul that he made. We have access to the cues that our emotions and bodies send us. We can get to the root of our longings, beliefs, and convictions. We can tap into our tremendous potential, even as we acknowledge our brokenness. We can develop trust in our strengths, which paradoxically gives us confidence to seek support for our growth areas.

But, as women, we don't often hear or see modeled what it's like to trust our God-given selves. We don't feel that we can trust ourselves, so we succumb to self-doubt. For example, you might find it challenging to trust yourself to

- make a decision that goes against what is expected of you,
- speak up for what you need or want in a relationship, or
- honor a signal your body is giving you.

Instead of trusting your own God-given instincts, you defer to people and cues outside you. But the problem with this way of thinking is, if you can't trust yourself, how can you trust anyone around you?

How can you know if another person is worthy of your trust if you don't first know how to recognize and respond to the cues your own soul and body are giving you?

It's a terrible place to find yourself. Instead of taking charge of the things you can, you search for answers outside of you or "hope" that God will bail you out. For example, you might react in these ways:

- Call every friend you can think of, hoping one of them will have the answer.
- Pray your boss will do right by you, even if he's been unethical in the past.
- Expect your spouse will somehow know what you need.
- Hope your toxic parents will suddenly change.
- Frantically scan the Bible—and Instagram—for inspiration.

Yes, sometimes God does send help in these ways. But sometimes God doesn't. Many times, God seems completely silent. Then what? How do you figure out how to get what you need in those situations?

When you don't trust yourself, you put yourself at the mercy of other people. Instead of using the abilities God gave you, you lean on others blindly. That's misusing the Bible to put you in a position of unhealthy dependency on other people.

The Consequence of Codependency

To put it even more bluntly, the reason you don't know how to trust yourself is that you were taught to be codependent. You never learned how to honor yourself because you were taught to focus only on other people. At best, this teaching is a naive oversight; at worst, it's a form of spiritual abuse.

As described in chapter 2 of this book, codependency is a pattern of relating in which you focus so much on others, you neglect the work of developing your own sense of self.

When you're taught that you can't trust yourself, you have no choice but to rely on other people to guide you. Furthermore, when you're taught to always put others first, you disregard your own needs.

Think about it. Taken together, these commonly taught messages leave you with the following two options to guide your decision-making:

1. Trust only other people. What do *they* think about what I need or want?
2. Put others first. What do *they* need and want?

Notice how there is no place for *you* in either of these options. You are focused on meeting other people's needs or looking to other people for permission. Your eyes are always on them. Nowhere in this equation is there a place for *you* to sort out who you are and what you want or need. This is not healthy spirituality. Instead, this is a church, our society, or your family teaching you to be codependent.

What harmful consequences does this teaching cause? Well, signs of codependency show up in the following ways:

- Hiding your needs so no one views you as a burden.
- Enabling or making excuses for someone else's dysfunctional behavior.
- Telling white lies to avoid any form of conflict.
- Relying excessively on others for decision-making.
- Discounting your own wants, needs, instincts, or convictions.

It's important to note that codependency exists on a spectrum. On one end of the spectrum are those who do not trust themselves at all. On the opposite end of the spectrum are those who don't trust anyone else, described as *counterdependency*. Sometimes people vacillate between the two extremes. Regardless, the goal is to move toward *healthy dependence*, which requires a strong sense of self *and* an ability to rely on other people.

Dear reader, are any of these dynamics occurring in your marriage, workplace, friendships, or family? It is crucial to pay attention to those interactions.

CODEPENDENCY	HEALTHY DEPENDENCE	COUNTER-DEPENDENCY
"You don't think I'm a bad person, right?"	"I'm struggling with guilt. Are you available to listen as I try to understand why?"	"I only answer to myself."
"I'll tell you what you want to hear. It's easier that way."	"I'd value the opportunity to talk this issue through with you."	"I'm all set. There's nothing to talk about."
"I need your permission."	"I don't need your permission, but I value your perspective."	"I don't care what you think."
"I can't be alone if you don't give me the validation I crave."	"I need time alone to cool off before circling back to this conversation."	"I take time alone so I never have to show vulnerability."
"I can't live without you."	"I'm better with you in my life."	"I don't need anyone."

Lest you think codependency shows up only in those who seem outwardly needy, consider these examples:

- A strong, independent man who can't say no to a family member
- A dynamic ministry leader who can't stand up to a staff member
- A successful executive who finds herself in a controlling romantic relationship

Codependency is not easily stereotyped. It operates insidiously, typically deep under the surface of our lives. It's closely linked to trauma. It's often reinforced in faith communities and in our culture. And we are masters at hiding it.

It's one thing to sacrifice in healthy ways for other people. It's another to betray yourself altogether. It's one thing to use the strength that you've gained to help a loved one to heal. It's another to bypass your own healing. When you neglect your own healing, you aren't living out of the fullness of who you are.

We become master deflectors, dodging criticism, shame, or rejection with a flip of a magic white lie. The mere hint of disapproval or anger sends us into a tailspin of activity:

- "No, no, I didn't mean that. I'm sorry! Really, you're great."
- "I'm not worried about the cost—I'll make it amazing."
- "What was I thinking? Of course I can babysit your kids and dog all next week."

We mindlessly meet needs around us—and we do it with skill and precision. But here's the rub: you are behaving out of your conditioning.

You might be making the other person feel good, but the real you is trapped deep inside. You become so good at pretending with others that they don't realize you've never once shared something genuine about yourself. After all, *you* barely realize it yourself. It's as if you've put that invisibility cloak on. You show up in the world, but no one can actually see you. And, while other people might like it when you play small, here's the problem: hiding your true self to make others happy keeps you stuck in relationships you don't really want.

If you camouflage your true self and always blend in, you can avoid conflict, bullying, pettiness, and resentment. But you also avoid intimacy, connection, and the joy of being known. Soon, you look around and realize how lonely you are. You might even be surrounded by other people. Yet no one really knows you. They only know the version of you that makes *them* feel okay.

At some point, you have to stop hiding, rip off that invisibility cloak, and start showing up in your life. But there is one more factor that makes this process incredibly chal-

Hiding your true self to make others happy keeps you stuck in relationships you don't really want.

lenging: in many cases, hiding your true self is part of a pact you have already made with somebody else.

The Contract of Codependent Relationships

Many people with codependent tendencies find themselves in codependent relationships—relationships built on the agreement that you will stay small. The "contract" that creates this type of relationship is often entered into unknowingly, especially at first.

For example, let's say someone is soft-spoken and timid. This person is drawn to another person who is blunt and decisive. They're attracted to each other's strengths, so they start spending time together. Over time, this relationship could develop into a healthy, mutually beneficial relationship. An unspoken agreement could be formed based on honesty and respect: each person understands their strengths and tends their own growth areas. Each one also seeks to bring out the best in the other.

But let's say the same two people come together with a different type of agreement. Neither person is aware of their wounds or conditioning. Instead of harnessing the power of the relationship to help them each become stronger, they bypass their healing work. They make a silent pact with each other: "I'll pretend not to see your harmful behaviors, if you pretend not to see mine." Initially, this feels good, maybe even euphoric. It might even feel like they "complete" each other. Over time, it almost always turns toxic.

Let's explore what that might look like between two common archetypes of a codependent relationship.

Type 1. The Helper

If you are the helper in this relational contract, you disregard your needs in order to support, please, or defer to the other person. Over time, you might feel consumed by the relationship, as if you can't get the space that you need. Or you might feel like you can't express what you really think. Often the solution offered to you is to set boundaries with the other person. But setting boundaries requires the ability to assert yourself. If you were conditioned to fawn, the very act of asserting yourself evokes anxiety. Furthermore, if the other person is abusive, it may not be wise. You find yourself looping a self-defeating cycle, like this:

- You're exhausted, worn out, feeling like a doormat.
- The thought of speaking up for what you need leaves you feeling anxious.
- You don't know how to do it, so you settle for the status quo.
- You beat yourself up for behaving like a doormat.

To cope, you reassure yourself that you're being "helpful," "useful," or "sacrificial." You try to push down the growing turmoil inside of you. Without realizing it, you disregard your own legitimate needs while enabling the other person to stay in their unhealthy patterns of behavior.

Type 2. The Controller

If you are a controller, you might be stuck in patterns of addiction, anger, control, or manipulation. Over time, you might feel as if the only way to get love is to control the other person. You might feel threatened if you sense any autonomy on their part—the slightest divergence feels like betrayal or even rejection. You can't tolerate the feelings of vulnerability it brings up. Maybe you were conditioned to "fight" when you feel fear. Instead of learning to face your pain honestly, you tell yourself that you're "special" or "necessary" for your partner's survival. You feel entitled to their loyalty. You might even become abusive in your quest to maintain control at all costs.

———

The relationship pattern is toxic, and both people have to heal. Both people are betraying critical aspects of themselves to keep the relationship together. Both people need to face their own wounds and work to develop a strong sense of self.

If only one person is willing to heal and the other is not, the relationship can't thrive. If that's been your experience, the good news is that *you* can still heal and move forward to create the healthy relationships you desire.

The difference between healthy and unhealthy dependence is the degree to which each person is willing to face—and heal—their own wounds. That's exactly what I started to realize after Joe (now my husband) called me out on the way I had been hiding myself.

Observing Painful Patterns

After the discussion in the restaurant with Joe, something shifted within me.

I began to observe myself in an entirely new way. A few weeks later, I showed up one night at a large gathering at our church. I watched myself smile, nod, and say the exact right thing to the person in front of me. I watched as each person walked away feeling cared for and seen.

There was only one problem. As I observed myself, I felt a tidal wave of emptiness wash over me. It was like I was watching some part of me win everybody over, even as what was happening felt unbelievably lonely. The disconnect between how I interacted with people and the loneliness inside me evoked unhealed pain from the past. I was observing myself fawning—I was pleasing every single person around me as I simultaneously became aware of how invisible *I* felt.

I was becoming aware of the pain of my youth, of the longing that I had buried for years to be seen for who I really was. I was watching myself put on my magical cloak of invisibility, the one that helped me contort and transform into whatever posture or facial expression the person in front of me wanted. I was watching myself play the game I'd been conditioned to play to get love:

- Smile
- Nod
- Compliment
- Laugh
- Don't be too loud
- Don't be too quiet
- Never make it about yourself

It was as if I'd been programmed to say and do exactly what the person in front of me needed.

I had thought this was being kind. I had told myself, "You're a nice person. It's your job to make others feel good."

But it didn't add up. Why did I feel so utterly wretched inside as I acted out what I had been taught was Christlike? I was watching myself exist as two different people: a woman who knew how to make everyone else feel great while an angst-ridden young girl lay buried and aching inside her. How had I missed this dichotomy?

I was betraying myself to please others.

I was betraying a precious child of God, a woman Jesus had come to make whole.

I was betraying myself, and I had been calling it Christlike.

In fact, I was observing my patterns with a fair amount of wonder. If that's not what God wanted from me, then what did God want?

Becoming the Best of You

I had to come out from hiding—to get to the root of myself and start living authentically.

Those are nice words to say, but they are painful to live, especially at first. As you take off the cloak of invisibility, you also take off all your ways of coping and surviving. Remember that tiny fawn curled up to stay safe in the wilderness? Initially, her legs are wobbly as she learns how to stand up on her own. She has to find her bearings before she grows strong.

Facing that tenderness inside can feel terribly vulnerable. It's painful to see the ways we learned to betray ourselves. We feel regret, embarrassment, or anger that we have to unlearn what we were taught. We feel like we should be further along. In some instances, it feels easier to go back to hiding. In fact, the process often evokes the ultimate adversary to our growth—shame.

The real driver underneath codependency is shame. In his wonderful book *The Soul of Shame*, psychiatrist Dr. Curt Thompson described how what he calls "evil's vector," shame, enters via childhood wounds and disrupts the person God wants you to become. It disrupts every single relationship you have, including the one you have with yourself.[12] Shame works to keep you stuck. It fans the flames of old wounds and toxic messages that tell you to stay hidden.

Let me be clear: shame is not constructive. It's not how God sees you, and it's not how God wants you to see yourself.

If shame shows up as you start to face areas of wounding, don't be surprised. Above all, do not be deterred. Leaving behind the old ways you've been taught can feel foreign and scary. You might even doubt if you're on the right path. The way you have stayed in relationships with other people hasn't always worked well, but at least you understood it.

Take heart, dear one.

This is the point at which you are starting to heal. You are unearthing old ways. You're reexamining how you've portrayed yourself and how you've shown up in your relationships with other people. And here's the good news: shame cannot tolerate the real you, who, armed with God's power, bravely faces the truth.

As I began to heal, I returned to that young girl inside me who had longed to be the Queen of Hearts back in sixth grade. I imagined sitting next to her as she shared her fear about getting up on stage and inhabiting such a strong, visible character. I tried to see her through God's eyes. I tried to see her as a loving parent would. I imagined a conversation that went something like this:

I know you're scared. I know you think you don't have what it takes. But some part of you knows you can do it. Some part of you has a fire that radiates tremendous power, whether you are loud or quiet.

I see you looking at everyone else around you, pointing out every single person's strengths. But stop for a moment. Take your eyes off them. Turn toward yourself for a moment.

What if no one—and I mean no one—can take your place?

What if you could dig into your own brave fire deep inside?

Your Queen won't look like anybody else. She's going to look like you. She might be self-contained and quiet, or she might be bold and over-the-top. She might lead with her vulnerability, or she might lead with her strength. But when she utters those words out of the pit of her belly, every single person will turn to pay attention.

Who you are is powerful. Now, get out there and inhabit the heck out of yourself.

You see, in order to become this Queen I admired, I had to become myself.

Dear friend, the same is true for you.

In the chapters to come, you'll learn how to heal past wounds, uncover your voice, and express your authentic self.

Reflections

1. When you look at the chart of codependency, where do you see yourself in it?
   - Do you see codependent tendencies in yourself? If so, what keeps you from moving toward healthy dependence on others?
   - Do you see counterdependent tendencies in yourself? If so, what keeps you from moving toward healthy dependence on others?
2. When have you noticed shaming messages? Start getting curious (vs. critical) about those messages. For example, consider:
   - What's an early memory of shame?
   - How did you cope with shame at the time?
   - In what ways does shame show up in your life today?

PART 2

Discover the Best of You

When we are born we bear the seeds of blight;
Around us life & death are torn apart,
Yet a great ring of pure and endless light
Dazzles the darkness in my heart.

—Madeleine L'Engle, *A Ring of Endless Light*

Chapter 4

What Am I Really Like?

Seeing Yourself as God Does

MY FRIENDS ARE COMPLETELY USELESS!" JACKIE BELLOWED, as if I was not sitting a few feet away from her. "Just yesterday, one of them told me I need to get over my divorce. Meanwhile, she sits in her perfect home, with her perfect life, with no clue what it's like for me."

"Jackie, I hear you," I said with steady calm, speaking more to the angry one within her—whom I was pretty sure had never felt heard—than to the volume of her voice. "I believe you, and I can tell how much you're hurting."

Jackie burst into tears: "No one gets it. No one knows how lonely I feel. I'm so sick of being angry all the time!"

"I hear you, Jackie." I said again. "I have great respect for the way you have survived some very painful things."

A single mother, Jackie had clawed her way to sanity after her husband left her alone and penniless. She was raising two teens, barely making ends meet while working full-time. It was hard to tell whom she was most angry at: herself, God, or the people who had let her down.

She was also angry with her oldest son, which was the main reason she'd come to see me. By all reports from his teachers, her son was a great kid, strong-willed yet bighearted. He had no interest in the status quo of the cool kids at school, yet he was respected. He was doing well in his classes. But according to Jackie, at home he could be stubborn and argumentative. He pushed back on Jackie's requests to pick up his room and get to bed at a certain time. In return, she doubled down, leading to angry standoffs between them. She was exhausted and wanted him to toe the line, but he was not about to be controlled. As a result, he and Jackie were constantly tangling over what, by all estimations, seemed to be minor issues.

As Jackie and I worked together, the facts of the situation become clearer.

- Jackie was angry.
- Jackie's son was not the primary issue.
- Jackie was praying a lot, but God was not magically taking her anger away.

Thankfully, Jackie was willing to consider that God might be inviting her into the work of healing. She agreed to take a break from tangling with her son—and her friends—and began to unpack her anger within the safety of my office. Her anger was what we call a *trailhead*.[1] It was a sign indicating a path she needed to go down. As Jackie gave voice to her anger, in the presence of a compassionate witness, its source started to become clear.

Jackie's dad had left her when she was very young to start an entirely new family far away, complete with a brand-new daughter. He was a maverick, but not in a constructive way. He'd recklessly charted his own course, without a care for who got hurt in the process.

Jackie was angry with her dad. But the truth was Jackie shared his maverick streak. She hated that part of herself—just like she hated it in her dad.

As a young girl, Jackie had been strong, smart, and unafraid to take a stand. When one of her peers did something she thought didn't make sense, she would point it out. This strategy didn't go so well for her when it came to being liked. She soon earned labels such as "rebellious" and "hard to get along with." Her peers liked to "poke the bear," as Jackie put it. She often gave them the reaction that they wanted.

Her mom told her to learn to be quiet and blend in with the other kids. But she couldn't do it. One day, when a girl in her math class made a snide remark about the outfit Jackie was wearing, she recalled feeling her face heat up and her heart start racing. She stood up, turned around, dumped the girl's books onto the floor, and left the room.

Jackie was given detention. The other girl was not punished. Her mom's response was to double down, determined to break her strong will, as the psychologist she was reading at the time recommended.

"If I could just learn to fit in, to be quiet—I'd have been okay. But I would get so angry. It's like I couldn't stop myself," Jackie told me as she reflected on her childhood.

Jackie had a fight response that was rooted both in how God made her and in how she'd been conditioned by the environment around her. She couldn't tolerate people who were hypocritical or mean. This was a beautiful quality—a spark God had put into her.

The problem was that Jackie's mom hadn't known how to reflect this quality back to Jackie and help her to harness it effectively. Instead of honoring this aspect of Jackie, she had tried to get her to become someone she was not. These attempts had backfired, only amplifying Jackie's feelings of being misunderstood and creating even more tension and anger inside her body.

Jackie had unknowingly arrived at the following conclusions, each one detrimental to her core sense of self:

- She didn't feel seen or understood by other people.
- She thought there was something deeply wrong with her.

Furthermore, as a result of not feeling seen by others and distrustful of herself, she had developed unhealthy patterns of relating:

- She resented other people.
- She wished to be somebody she was not.

Each of these core wounds inhibited her ability to thrive. Instead of having a strong sense of herself, she was bound by the voice of shame and stuck in a constant state of fight or flight. To cope, she would bitterly pick other people apart. At the same time, though, she desperately wished to be more like them.

Jackie couldn't see herself clearly. As a result, she couldn't draw strength from who she was at her core. She didn't know her inherent worth and the reality of her potential.

Instead of seeing herself as wonderfully made and capable, Jackie saw herself through the lens of "not enough" and "bad." She had unknowingly built her identity through the reflection of a broken mirror. This broken mirror showed her only shattered fragments of her wounding.

And now Jackie was in jeopardy of holding this same broken mirror up to her son. To break this cycle, she was going to have to grieve her own pain, heal her past, and learn to show up as the woman she really was.

Will the Real You Please Stand Up?

Your real identity is not a list of personality traits, your Enneagram type, or a list of all your top strengths, though these things are helpful to understand.[2] Your true self develops out of the following four psychological and spiritual roots:

1. I am safe.
2. I am seen.
3. I have purpose.

4. No one can take my place on this earth.

When you know deep inside that you are safe and seen, that you have purpose, and that no one else can take your place on this earth, you will be well on your way to a life of connection and authentic expression. It doesn't matter if you're loud and bold or whether you're quiet and shy. It doesn't matter what specific gifts you have or the challenges that you face. You know in your soul that you are God's beloved child, a walking masterpiece. You are a living, breathing glimpse of heaven.

Unfortunately, this knowing doesn't happen automatically. Most people aren't born with a deep sense of confidence and clarity about who they are. Instead, children need a healthy environment and guidance at key junctures to develop a strong sense of self over time.

In fact, renowned psychologist Erik Erikson identified eight stages of identity development, each one representing a milestone you must overcome. These eight stages highlight that becoming your true self is a process that spans an entire lifetime.

1. Infancy: trust versus mistrust
2. Early childhood: autonomy versus shame and doubt
3. Preschool: initiative versus guilt
4. School age: industry versus inferiority
5. Adolescence: identity versus role confusion
6. Young adulthood: intimacy versus isolation
7. Middle adulthood: generativity versus stagnation
8. Maturity: integrity versus despair[3]

As fascinating as all these milestones are, in my role as a counselor, most of my work involves helping women heal from wounds at the initial stages, all the way back in childhood. I have boiled these first four stages down into two key elements: *connectedness* and *authenticity*.

Let's examine how these two elements affect the way you view yourself.

Connectedness: Safe and Seen

Being Safe

When a tiny baby is held in loving arms, she experiences safety in her body and in the depths of her soul. Even though she can't remember it in her conscious mind, this experience of physical and emotional security is foundational to a strong sense of self.

If her caregivers nurture and comfort her, providing her with healthy touch, she develops what psychologists call *secure attachment*. She has a foundational experience of another human as trustworthy. She absorbs deep inside her body what it's like to be safe, held, and soothed by someone else.[4]

On the other hand, if she doesn't experience a secure attachment with a primary caregiver, she doesn't know what safety feels like. She might find it difficult to distinguish between people she can trust and those she can't. Her internal alert system moves into survival mode, and over time she learns to cope with anxious feelings through fighting, fleeing, freezing, or fawning. *This is not her fault.*

Being Seen

In addition to experiencing safety with someone else, a child also needs to become aware of her independence, her autonomy. A healthy sense of autonomy comes *after* secure attachment. As a baby becomes a toddler, she begins to explore the world around her. But she's not yet ready to do this alone—she explores her independence while remaining connected to a safe, supportive caregiver. As a result, she feels *seen*.

But what if she isn't seen in this way? It's a common experience for many. Maybe her caregivers ignore or neglect her. As a result, she learns to doubt her worth. She feels invisible. Or maybe they shame or hurt her. As a result, her sense of herself is distorted. She absorbs a feeling of rejection or being unlovable. *This is not the view God has of her.*

Taken together, these two formative experiences of being safe and being seen set the stage for how you experience *connectedness*, both in relationship to others and to yourself.

Connectedness is a beautiful dance of togetherness and apartness, dependence, and autonomy. Connectedness is the opposite of codependency. It's knowing you belong to others, even as, paradoxically, you belong deeply to yourself.[5] It's how I believe God made us to exist in relationship with other people. And it's how I believe that God relates to us as well.

In addition to your early caregivers, the wider culture has an impact on your sense of connectedness as you move through life, both in negative and positive ways. You can have loving parents and still be influenced by toxic systems in the world around you. For example, if you grow up in an environment that perpetuates racism, misogyny, or any abuse of power, your sense of connectedness gets wounded.[6]

The reverse is also true. You may have been neglected by your parents only to encounter someone trustworthy outside your immediate family, someone who made you feel safe or seen. For example, you may have discovered safety in an adoptive parent, a grandparent, church group, teacher, friend, or a neighboring family. As a result, you stumbled upon a healing balm. Glimpses of safety in another person reveal what safety feels like inside of you.

Your body relaxes; your shoulders untense. Good chemicals course through your brain, releasing serotonin, dopamine, and even oxytocin, a hormone that bonds two people together. Your soul experiences something it recognizes as healing. It says, "I want more of *this*." You catch a glimpse of what it's like to move from a survival state within your body into a deeper sense of your truest, God-made self. And you learn to rely on that internal gauge to guide you as you discern future relationships.

> **Glimpses of safety in another person reveal what safety feels like inside of you.**

In Jackie's case, her dad's abandonment had wounded her sense of connectedness. She experienced herself as invisible and alone. She constantly pushed people away, even as she yearned for someone to hold her close. Her push-pull way of relating stemmed from that young girl inside, desperate to be seen. As we worked together, Jackie connected to the pain she still carried. Slowly, her soul began to respond to the safety our relationship provided. She felt what it was like to be known and seen at the deepest levels. Her fight response began to soften, and she began to experience what connection feels like.

Like Jackie, you were designed to heal in the context of loving relationship. You can lose yourself as a result of relationships, and you can also find yourself through the power of relationships. As you experience what it's like to be safe with and seen by someone who is trustworthy, you connect more deeply to your truest, God-made self.

Authenticity: Purpose and Confidence

Having Purpose

As a child enters school she starts to expand her world. She plays more with other children and spends time away from home. She finds herself drawn to certain types of activities and individuals. As she begins to take more initiative, healthy caregivers ideally provide guidance, helping her to understand herself. For example, she might learn that she is great at art but struggles with making friends. The adults around her help her make sense of both her strengths and her challenges.

Imagine a child who is guided through this season well. She can recognize and cultivate her strengths. She also learns how to navigate challenges and disappointment, gaining a sense of resilience. She knows how to identify her preferences. She develops a sense of purpose.

But if this young girl moves into this stage without anyone to guide her, she is left to make sense of complex challenges on her own. Shame, guilt, and doubt creep in, tainting her self-perception. She picks up faulty beliefs about her worth and potential.

Having Confidence

As a child progresses through school, she begins to gauge her competence. She starts getting grades and tries out different hobbies such as sports and music. She becomes increasingly aware of how her own performance at school, both academically and socially, stacks up against her peers. This is such a critical time for parents and teachers to help this young girl formulate how she thinks about herself. Ideally, she gains a sense of confidence in the unique gifts she has to contribute.

But in the absence of guidance, she may start to think of herself as inferior to other people. For example, if she is bullied by other children or struggles in school, she might ingest painful messages such as *I'm less-than*, or *There's nothing special about me.*[7] She might start comparing herself to others and struggle to see her own strengths. Instead of leaning into the important work of honoring how God made *her*, she might wish to be somebody else. This is a wound she can heal.

Constantly comparing yourself to others is a cue that you've disconnected from your own sense of self.

Taken together, these second two formative stages—purpose and confidence—help you establish a sense of *authenticity*. In other words, you develop a sense of who you are and you learn to claim it. You understand your own strengths and you accept your limitations. You don't wish to be someone else—you understand that *no one can take your place.*

Authenticity is rooted in the biblical idea that God made you to reflect who God is in a unique and beautiful way. Some of what makes you who you are is related to your DNA, your neurological makeup, and a few inherent personality traits[8]—what psychologists call *nature*. Some of the unique essence of you is shaped by the environment into which you were born, your family, and your culture—what psychologists call *nurture*. These aspects of your story are yours to understand, honor, and, in many cases, heal. Your identity isn't fixed. It's a process of bringing out the best of you.

For example, maybe you're stubborn. Maybe you're shy. Maybe you can run fast or hear the chords of a song without even trying. In Jackie's case, she was strong-willed. She didn't suffer fools. This quality was a part of her God-given nature. It was also a quality that didn't comply with her mother's wishes or line up with what her peers thought was cool.

In our work together, I helped Jackie regain a sense of purpose and confidence in her own gifts. God put that fire in her. She was never going to become quiet and demure. That's not how God made her. God had given her passion, sharp wit, and yes, a bit of her own father's maverick streak. She needed to learn how to honor those aspects of herself and use them for her own good and for the good of other people. We discussed the many places in the Bible where Jesus grew angry and even overturned some tables, not unlike how Jackie had. We discussed how Jesus' fire was always wise and well-directed. He never wielded it cruelly, but with a sense of justice.[9]

As Jackie slowly began to accept her fire as a God-given part of who she was, something beautiful happened. Instead of reacting out of her fight-response conditioning, she started to pause and check within. She began to get curious about a fiery impulse *before* jumping into an angry battle with her son.

As you commit to the work of becoming who you really are in partnership with God, you reclaim lost parts of you and learn to lead yourself wisely. You also learn how to build the close, healthy relationships with other people God made us to enjoy.

I Before We

Here's what is critical to understand when it comes to establishing relationships as an adult: *identity* is necessary for *intimacy*. This means that a healthy sense of self is vital to creating healthy relationships with other people.[10] In fact, in Erikson's framework, a stable sense of self grows out of years of cultivating deep roots, as you seek to understand your purpose, challenges, and the gifts you have to bring. It's out of this strong sense of self that you learn the meaning of what Erikson calls "fidelity"—or faithfulness—the ability to commit yourself to other people and to the world around you with integrity.

It's hard to demonstrate faithfulness to others if you don't understand how to be faithful to yourself. Furthermore, faithfulness to yourself shows faithfulness to the One who made you.

Faithfulness to yourself involves

- understanding what you need to thrive;
- prioritizing the care of your mind, heart, body, and soul; and
- honoring the unique gifts God has given you.

Faithfulness to someone else involves

- understanding what they need to thrive;
- prioritizing the care of their mind, heart, body, and soul; and
- honoring the unique gifts God has given them.

Both matter deeply. One cannot exist without the other. It's difficult to show up faithfully for someone else if you don't also know how to show up for yourself. But most people don't arrive at adulthood with a strong sense of self. And, to complicate the situation, most people enter into their most important relationships with other people before healing their own sense of self.

Do you see why codependency is such an epidemic? Instead of seeking to heal ourselves first, we jump right into relationships as a cure for all that hurts.

How does this land on you? Did you experience yourself as safe and seen, as having purpose and confidence? Did you have a strong sense of fidelity to your God-given self as you entered into adulthood?

If not, take comfort that you're not alone. In fact, I know that I didn't. But I've learned the power of claiming who I am. And so can you.

Here is what I know to be true: if you're willing to face yourself honestly, including areas of pain, you can heal your core sense of self. The beauty of this work yields incredible results: as you heal yourself, you start to create the relationships you crave.

I'm not saying every relationship will magically fall into place. But I am saying that as you heal yourself, you will start to discover the kind of people that you truly want and need to bring into your life. And you will learn how to show up faithfully, in a way that honors others, God, *and* yourself. Healing starts by saying, "I want to see what you see, God. I want to become more of my true self with your help."[11]

The Mirror of Truth

Imagine if God held a mirror up and said, "This is who you really are." In that mirror, God would show you the wonders of your strength, your sincerity, or the way you care for other people. God might show you how thoughtful you are. He might highlight your persistence or the way you hate injustice. Or he might show you a moment when your kindness melted someone else's sadness. You might see yourself walking bravely into a room full of people, feeling like a nobody. But in God's mirror, you see a valiant soul, a light-bearer, someone who reveals to others who God is.

As your trust builds, God also starts to show you a few things that are hard. Maybe in that mirror, God reflects to you a moment when you lied or shoved someone else aside. Maybe you let bitterness bring out the worst of you and you took your own pain out on someone else. Maybe you turned away from opportunities to be brave. It's painful to see this reflection. But here's the important distinction: God's mirror, while honest, does not include shame. Instead, you feel sorrow because it's not the person you want to be.[12]

God holds up the mirror *not* to hurt you but to point you to a better way.

Can you imagine seeing yourself as God sees you—as the best version of yourself *and* in some of your very worst moments? Can you imagine that honest reflection without the presence of shame?

This is what Jackie learned to do with unbelievable courage and persistence. Over time, as Jackie saw herself as God did—both in her strength and in the harm her anger could cause—she began to heal wounds from her past. She grieved the dad she never knew and even caught a glimpse of who he might have been had he faced and healed his own pain. As a result, she started to see herself more clearly—the fierce yet tender woman she had been all along.

She also saw her son more clearly. One day, several months into our work together, Jackie went to her son and said something like this:

> "Danny, I'm so sorry. I've not been parenting you well. I've not been seeing who you are and understanding your unique gifts and challenges. I'm committed to growing and doing the work to become the parent that you need me to be, with God's help."

Over time, Jackie backed up her apology with actions. She used the new understanding about herself to parent her own son out of the best of who she was. He needed her to honor his own maverick streak while helping him to guide it. He needed her to help him become the best version of who he was—to parent out of creativity and vision instead of from her own fears and unhealed pain.

Jackie's story taught me something that I've never forgotten: The best of you does not equal perfection. The best of you sees yourself honestly and admits when you've gotten it wrong.

As a result, you help others become the best of who they are too.

This is exactly what God is trying to do with all of us. I don't think

God is randomly sending feel-good platitudes our way. Nor do I think God is trying to shrink us down or squash our sense of self.

I think God *sees* us.

God sees who we have been in the past.

God sees who we are right now.

God also sees the best of who we can become.

The best of you sees yourself honestly and admits when you've gotten it wrong.

And what if there is no shame in any of this, no matter where you've been?

What if you could see yourself as God does?

What if who you are reflects who God is in a unique and precious way?

Could you read that sentence again—aloud to yourself?

What if who I am reflects who God is in a unique and precious way?

Look in this mirror of truth for one moment, this mirror that God holds up to show you who you are. Do you see what I see? A beautiful soul braving your way through the holy work of healing? It's time for *you* to begin to see yourself in this way.

At the core of who we are, being seen—and *loved*—as we really are is exactly what we long for. In fact, our most important job on this earth is to learn how to see ourselves as God does.[13]

Honor the *I* Inside of You

Becoming your true self is not a destination you arrive at in your mind. It's a process of waking up to who you are and what is truly happening inside. It starts with paying attention.

I have come to believe that learning to pay attention to yourself is holy, sacred work that matters not only for the health of your soul but for the health of all your relationships, including your relationship with God. This is the work I have committed my life to—the work of helping you go deeper into becoming your truest self in God.

Take a moment right now, right where you are, and consider the following questions:

- Does your body feel loose or tense?
- Is your breath moving deep into your belly?
- Are you aware of an emotion?
- Do you sense any mental distractions?

As you engage your senses and notice what is happening in your immediate sphere of awareness, you are becoming aware of your *I*. It's the center of who you are. It's the core of your being.

I is who you are when you are most present to yourself. It's you when you're fully engaged, fully alive, fully aware in any given moment. *I* is who you are as you exist in your own body. *I* is aware of what you're feeling right now, even if it's crummy.

If you want to be part of something bigger than yourself—a relationship, a family, or a movement—you have to show up exactly as you are. You have to honor the *I* inside you.

Here's the kicker: whether you're consciously aware of it or not, your *I* holds tremendous power. When your *I* shows up, it changes everything around you. *I* changes the energy in the room that you're in right now. *I* changes the composition of your family, your neighborhood, your community. When you show up at an office, your church, or at your child's school, your *I* changes that room.

I matters.

And while I do understand that there is no *I* in *team*, I want you to hear me say: there is no team if *you* do not show up to play your role on it. There is no "we" if you are not doing your part to bring yourself into the relationship or the community.

Let me be clear: your *I* doesn't have to be the boldest, the loudest, or the flashiest in order to matter.

In fact, your *I* might be the fire of silence blazing inside. It might be the calm ripples of quiet confidence, aware that your presence matters. It might be the courage to sit in a room full of people all by yourself—peaceful, observing, curious—waiting to see who is drawn to you. Or it might be the courage to stand up in front of a crowd and let yourself loose in a bold declaration.

Consciousness of your *I* is the most powerful tool you have. It's more powerful than size, looks, charisma, or talent. Consciousness of your *I* is the power you wield in every single situation, whether it's parenting your teen or standing up to a bully.

Becoming more of your true self doesn't mean becoming like the person you think you ought to be. Becoming your true self means allowing the powerful reality of who you are to be seen.

As you become more aware of your own self—mind, heart, and body—you become more aware of God. God meets you in the truth of who you are. And you start to find your voice.

Reflections

1. When have you felt safe with someone? Who or what makes you feel seen?
2. When did you last feel a sense of purpose or confidence in yourself?
3. What do you like about yourself?
4. What is your sense of how God sees you?

Chapter 5

How Do I Find My Voice?

Learning to Trust Yourself

THE INVITATION TO THE WORK OF FINDING YOUR VOICE CAN
show up in some not-so-pleasant ways, especially at first.

Gina learned this the hard way.

A mom of three, having barely turned forty, Gina had been living on autopilot, wide awake to her responsibilities yet asleep to the
alarms going off inside her body. She was an expert at perfecting her
way through raising three boisterous kids and managing her family's
thrift store business. In addition, she was the peacekeeper between
her mom and dad, where a lifetime of conflict had come to a painful head.

Despite Gina's best efforts to keep going strong, a voice of anxiety
had erupted seemingly out of nowhere. Her life had become like a painful maze. No matter what corner she rounded or what path she tried, a
wall of dread smacked her in the face. She couldn't figure out what was

happening. She only knew that she wanted out of this maze, but all her best efforts kept making it worse. She was stuck.

A part of her wanted to run far, far away from everything in her life. Instead, she'd contacted me for an appointment in my office.

She explained that the anxiety had started as she did seemingly normal things. "I was having coffee with a friend who was telling me about challenges in her marriage. I tried to listen to her, but I started having trouble breathing. My heart started racing, and I felt like the room was starting to spin. I made up a lame excuse to leave. Later, I tried to call my mom to talk, but she just kept complaining about my dad, which gave me knots in my stomach. I couldn't listen to her, so I hung up. Next thing I know, I'm lying on the floor sobbing like a ten-year-old."

I noticed that the common thread in Gina's encounters with anxiety had to do with having a task to complete or a person to help. So I asked her to focus on herself for a moment. "Gina, what are *you* feeling inside as you tell me all this?"

"I just feel so helpless," Gina said. "I can't fix anything. I can't fix my job. I can't fix my parents. I can't fix my friend. I can't even fix the stupid dishwasher that isn't working."

As I listened to Gina, something struck me as she worked her way through her list.

She was hurting.

She was exhausted.

She was overworked.

Yet she had not placed herself on her list of all that needed mending.

"What if *you* are the one who needs your attention, Gina? What if your anxiety is a clue that some part of *you* is in need of care?"

As I shared with her this reflection, Gina's body unclenched a bit. She started crying like that ten-year-old girl, lonely and bereft. As she sat there on my couch, her mind and body broken from all her efforts to mend everyone around her, her eyes locked with mine, and an almost inaudible voice came up from deep inside her: "I feel like that little boy who put his finger in the dike to hold back the floodwaters. Only I'm holding an entire ceiling up. I'm so tired of holding the ceiling up. But I don't know how to let it fall."

"I can help you let that ceiling fall, Gina," I said. "It's a great place to start."

As I worked with Gina over the following months, it was clear that she hadn't started holding the ceiling up as an adult. She'd learned to take on way too much responsibility as a young child. As a result, Gina had no clue how and when to take a day off—let alone what to do with herself if she did. She didn't know how to tend to herself when she felt knots in her stomach. Plus, she didn't know how to grieve or feel sad over the conflict in her parents' marriage. When it came to friendships, Gina wasn't sure what kind of people helped bring *her* back to life.

Over time, we worked together to help her find her way out of the painful maze her life had become. I helped her identify the conditioned voices she'd picked up, such as ego and shame. And she began to recognize new voices she'd silenced, such as painful feelings and even the voice of her body.

You find your voice by learning to hold your ear close to the ground of your own life. You listen for that tiny whisper of what gives you life.

She started to notice what made her stomach hurt, jaw clench, and her breathing go shallow. She learned to turn toward what made her body feel strong and well-tended. And she became aware of her own feelings and the messages they were sending. Most importantly, she learned to listen for the tenderness inside that needed her love, guidance, and protection.

She learned what we all have to learn: you find your voice by learning to hold your ear close to the ground of your own life. You listen for that tiny whisper of *what gives you life.*

Quieting the Ego

Have you ever had these types of thoughts flash through your mind?

- *Do not show that weakness.*
- *You must get their approval.*
- *You can't let them see the real you.*
- *She's doing that better than you.*

What is the common denominator within these statements? *Ego.*

Living in service of ego is exhausting.

Ego is the part of us that if left unfettered leads us toward the worst of who we are. Ego is completely in service of self-preservation. Furthermore, ego is fragile and shows you who you are only through the mirror of comparison with other people. Ego constantly scans the environment to determine how what you want stacks up against what other people will think.[1]

The voice of ego is sneaky. For example, it might be aware that you really want people to think you're smart. At the same time, it knows that your friends might judge you if you brag about your accomplishments. So ego comes up with a solution: it prompts you to humblebrag, allowing you to satisfy your urge for attention while appearing as if you don't care.

Don't get me wrong; we need to protect ourselves socially to some degree. But here's the problem: when your ego is in charge, instead of showing up authentically, you work to manage the perceptions of other people.

Living according to your ego keeps you trapped in creating a false version of yourself, within the armor of invisibility. You stay stuck trying to earn their approval instead of focusing on the more important work of staying true to the person God made you to be. It's the opposite of freedom, and it does not get you the authentic relationships you crave.

The voice of ego is further amplified by the world around us. It's magnified exponentially by social media, where numbers and likes tell us who's okay. It comes from trendy churches that replicate the high school popularity game by curating an "in" group and putting them onstage. It comes from gurus who pitch their unique story as something that "could be yours too." Instead of encouraging you to see yourself through God's mirror, they hold *themselves* up as the mirror, essentially saying, "You should be like me."

These messages tap into the wounded places deep within our souls, the parts of us that have bought the lie that we're not as good as other people. Ego tells us that the way to finally feel good is to work for their approval. But there's a catch: when you construct an identity based on comparison to others, you not only hurt yourself; you also stop seeing them accurately.

Unknowingly, you put someone else on a pedestal they have no business being on. Instead of doing your own work, you fixate on the lives of other people. Ego sits on your shoulder and whispers, *She's better than you. You should be who she is.*

If you look for it, you'll see that this voice has been with you most of your life. It's the part of you that surveys the landscape and tells you how amazing everybody else is. As a child, this voice likely got loud right around middle school. If no one helped you learn how to quiet this voice and find a truer path, ego can stay loud within you as you enter adulthood.

The key to quieting the voice of ego is to become aware of it. Awareness allows for what psychologists call *differentiation*, a process of separating your true self from a thought or feeling you are having.[2] When you differentiate from a thought or feeling inside your mind, you can observe it and learn more about the story it is telling you. Is this a story from past wounding? Is it one that's no longer serving you? Is it possible that it's time to create a different story?[3]

As you become aware of ego's voice, you can learn to gently counter it with God's help. Here are some examples:

VOICE OF EGO	VOICE OF THE BEST OF YOU
Do not show that weakness.	*My tenderness is a gift.*
You must get their approval.	*I'm living from integrity.*
You can't let them see the real you.	*I want to be known as I really am.*
She's doing that better than you.	*No one can take my place.*

Tending to the Tender Voice

As you quiet the voice of ego, you'll become aware of another voice inside. This tender voice speaks to the sadness, loneliness, or fear that all humans experience. It's a voice you may not want to hear, a voice you may have tried to silence. But your job is to listen for the tender voice and heal any painful stories it may carry.

As an adult, you still carry every prior version of yourself through the power of your memory. For instance, you carry the child who was once a baby and cried when you were hungry or uncomfortable. You carry the kid who walked into the first day of kindergarten and survived fifth grade. You carry the teen who made sense of high school and learned how to deal with parents, siblings, teachers, and peers. Each of these versions of you holds countless stories, countless memories of how you took yourself to be. Some of these stories are happy ones. Some of them are so painful that you've buried them far away. Whether these memories are happy or sad, they connect to a tender part of you who needs your care and attention.

This tender voice is more distant—harder to recognize. She hasn't been taught to speak up in your mind. In fact, her voice has been drowned out by ego and shame. She speaks to you through flashes of memories, or she speaks to you in subtle urges that don't always make sense. Your job is to learn to listen for her, because she is absolutely precious.

Her tender voice will lead you to remember parts of you that you've forgotten. She will also lead you to parts of you that need to be found, rescued, and healed from painful traumas.

Jesus spoke up directly about the value of vulnerable children and their example of authenticity. His words are helpful to remember.

The people brought children to Jesus, hoping he might touch them. The disciples shooed them off. But Jesus was irate and let them know it: "Don't push these children away. Don't ever get between them and me. These children are at the very center of life in the kingdom. Mark this: Unless you accept God's kingdom in the simplicity of a child, you'll never get in." Then, gathering the children up in his arms, he laid his hands of blessing on them.[4]

Imagine yourself as a young child in this scene. What does it feel like to hear adults shooing you away? Then, what does it feel like to hear Jesus call you in close to him?

This is how Jesus wants *you* to treat the tenderness within. Yet so often we're the ones shooing that voice away, as if it is a bother, burden, or problem to be solved. Instead, look to Jesus as your example, as he reminds you, *This is who matters most—the tender one.*

Often this teaching gets misconstrued to encourage us not to grow or develop into maturity. Many of my clients have been taught to think that staying like a child means that they should stay weak, dependent, and, frankly, uneducated or ignorant about their own hearts or bodies. But this is not what Jesus meant.

Instead, Jesus teaches us to honor what is tender, vulnerable, and innocent—in others and in ourselves. Where we are the most tender is where we're closest to holy ground.[5] It's where we're closest to him. And it's where we're closest to the truest version of ourselves.

This is what my client Gina began to do. As she looked for a way out of her painful maze, I asked her what she feared might happen if she stopped working so hard for other people. She grew quiet and tears streamed down her cheeks. "It sounds funny," she shrugged self-consciously, "but no one ever helped me learn to be a kid. It's almost like if I stopped working, I wouldn't know what to do with myself."

Gina told me that she was extremely conscientious as a child. No one tried to get to know her beyond her quiet, competent exterior. Ego told her that responsibility was the way to earn the love of other people. But the tears that streamed down her face told a different story. They suggested the presence of a young girl inside who longed to be seen and known apart from her conscientious personality.

When I asked Gina to tell me more about what her tears were saying, she answered my question with a memory. Her usually tense body visibly relaxed as she told me about a third-grade teacher who'd taught her class how to build a garden. For some reason, kicking off her shoes and putting her fingers and toes in the dirt while traipsing along behind this teacher had felt like pure joy to her.

As an adult, Gina hadn't made any time for gardening because there wasn't space for it in her busy life. But within a week of our meeting, she'd blocked off a section of her yard and started breaking open the ground. When I asked her how it felt to dig into that soil, she told me it felt thrilling. For those few precious minutes, her anxiety was gone. She was sweaty and dirty, but she'd caught a glimpse of a playful, joyful side of herself.

The tender voice inside you might not lead to gardening. It might lead you to a therapist's office to unpack a painful memory that feels too big to carry by yourself. It might walk you into a church again, because it remembers the goodness you experienced there. Or it might prompt you to walk out for a season . . . in order to heal yourself.

I can't say what the first step will be for you. You're as special and unique as that young girl buried inside of you. I can't tell you what she needs. But I can point you toward her voice.

Imagine yourself as a child, with an invitation to all the warmth and safety you could possibly need. If it's hard to imagine yourself as a child, then imagine a child who you know and love. It could be one of your own children, or it might be a niece, nephew, or grandchild.

What does this young one need? What do you long for her to have that she didn't receive?

Don't be surprised if parts of you aren't ready yet to find her. You've learned to keep her far away. Listening for her takes time.

But as you learn to hear her voice, you'll discover that she may well be the purest, most authentic thing about you. She's the one who cries when she's sad and asks to be held without feeling shame about it. She reveals your laughter and your curiosity—she wants to play, dance, sing, or be silly. You might notice that she's feisty or doesn't care what other people think.

She has a lot to teach you as you start to listen for her.

The Seduction of Shame

As you begin to hear this tender voice, shame is always lurking, waiting to shut down any new sign of life you are finding. Shame is the voice that tries to disrupt any movement toward healing. But you've grown wiser now; you're learning to recognize shame's voice and not let it derail you.

For example, as Gina listened for the tender voice inside, she began to create more space for rest and play. But she also started noticing a shaming voice well up in her mind:

What a waste of time. Who do you think you are?

She learned that the voice of shame doesn't necessarily mean you've done something wrong. The voice of shame might mean you're doing something vulnerable, valuable, and brave.

The voice of shame might mean you're doing something vulnerable, valuable, and brave.

When you step out with courage, speak up honestly, or let yourself be seen, it's normal to feel awkward or uncomfortable initially. But that's when shame steps in to fill in the details of a painful story that never got healed. When you were young, you felt vulnerable when you tried new activities or explored socially. That younger you might not have heard a supportive adult say things like

- "I'm proud of you."
- "You took a risk. That's courageous."
- "That was hard. It's makes sense that you feel tender."

In the absence of a loving witness, shame becomes the way you make sense of discomfort or uncertainty. You start to believe things like

- *I've made a fool of myself.*
- *I'm bad. That's why they didn't choose me.*
- *I must have done something wrong if I feel this way.*

The truth is, it can seem easier to feel shame than grieve the reality of the support you needed but didn't get. It's painful to face those wounds. But while the voice of shame tries to keep you hidden, revealing painful stories within a safe, loving relationship helps you grow strong and big inside. Remember, Jesus laid loving hands on those who were hurting. He would not let them be shamed.

In order to ward off shame's seduction, you have to learn to recognize its voice. This process can seem like a paradox: If you hide shame, it's emboldened. When you recognize shame for what it is, it's disempowered. For example, shame tells you

- *You're a terrible person.*
- *You're not worthy of love.*
- *You deserve this bad thing that's happened.*
- *You're making a fool of yourself.*
- *Who do you think you are?*

When you notice any voice of self-loathing, say, *Wait a minute, is this shame?*

If it is, name it. Extend compassion toward yourself. Then ask someone you trust to come alongside you to help take away its sting. Shame researcher Brené Brown said that "because shame is a social concept—it happens between people—it also heals best between people."[6] Shame is insidious. But here's the good news: shame dissipates when it's exposed to

- love
- curiosity
- compassion
- authenticity
- delight in who you are

When you heal shame, your mind has more capacity, more access to the best of who you are. Your nervous system relaxes, and you open up more pathways to creativity, curiosity, and play.[7] For example, instead of feeling shamed and lashing out, you might find yourself playfully teasing your teenager in response to their attempts to jab. Instead of defensiveness, you might notice brave, authentic words coming out in response to a prying question.

Identifying and naming shame is a key step on this path toward healing. Shame might not disappear right away—or forever—but you can learn to get distance from it. As you learn that you have what it takes to face shame, you gain confidence and courage.

Your Feelings Are a Factor

When I ask my clients about the emotions they experience because of something hard they are facing, they often start their sentences like this:

"I feel like she is so selfish!"

"I feel like they don't understand me!"

"I feel like he needs to get his act together!"

Here's a tip from a therapist: Those aren't feelings. Those are lingering traces of codependency. Statements that focus on other people tend to come from a part of you that has learned to cope with your pain by avoiding it.

Instead, a feeling would be something like this:

- I feel misunderstood.
- I feel frustrated by their silence.
- I feel discounted, like I don't matter.
- I feel angry.
- I feel hurt.
- I feel lonely.
- I feel unseen.

Notice the difference. It's much more vulnerable to describe your experience in terms of how it makes *you* feel inside.

It may bother you to get to the root of these feelings. It may feel vulnerable, or it might even feel self-indulgent. In fact, many of you were taught that your feelings are something to deny, pray away, or overcome. You may have been taught that facts are more important or to focus only on your faith.

Sure, we live in a culture where people blatantly disregard facts all the time. We live in a culture of spin and deception, a culture of gaslighting.

Facts matter.

And so do feelings.

Your emotions aren't *the* truth. But what you feel is *a* truth.

And it is a truth that matters.

When I asked Gina about her feelings, she looked at me like a deer in the headlights. She had never really thought about her emotions, let alone felt them. She went straight to the facts.

- "My mom is hurting."
- "My friend is in pain."
- "My business isn't doing well this month."

Gina was also good at leaning on her faith: "God will help me through it."

These facts were all true, and her faith was intact. But they were only two-thirds of the story. As I worked with Gina, she slowly began to face the truth of what she was feeling:

- "I'm scared."
- "I'm overwhelmed."
- "I'm exhausted."

Gina needed to face these painful feelings to deal with the facts of her situation better. Her feelings helped lead her to a better way of approaching the problems around her. The fact of her business was something she had to deal with right away. But the fact that her mom and friend were hurting was not something Gina needed to make a priority, despite what her conditioning had taught her. And while I had no doubt God was with Gina, I also ventured a guess that God wanted Gina to learn how to ask for help from other people.

Feelings must be held in tension with facts and with faith. The three go together. If I could submit a picture of the relationship between these three elements, it would look like this:

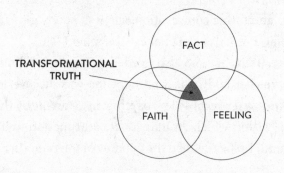

Emotional truth is simply acknowledging what you feel inside, whether it's justified or not. What you feel may not be based on fact at all. But the fact remains that you feel it.

It's not honest to tell yourself, "I'm not lonely," if you are, in fact, feeling lonely.

It's dishonest to tell someone else, "I'm not angry," if you are actually angry.

And it's dishonest to pretend you have no feelings of sorrow when a part of you is silently grieving. Feelings are what make you human. In fact, the best example of someone who demonstrated a full range of emotions is Jesus.

Acknowledging what you feel leads to emotional maturity. It doesn't mean that you automatically act on what you feel or demand validation for it. In later chapters of this book we'll discuss constructive ways to speak up on behalf of what you feel. But listening to what you feel inside is a crucial part of piecing together the larger puzzle of your life.

Your Body Is a Guide

A few weeks into my work with Gina, she mentioned that a friend who often sought her out for emotional support called to invite her for coffee. Gina said she noticed her stomach clench and her breathing grow shallow. This time, she paid attention. She heard herself say, "Beth, I'm so sorry. I actually have a lot on my own plate right now. I'm going to need to take a rain check."

As Gina told me about this conversation, she was nearly giddy. "I can't *believe* I said that. But I also can't believe the relief I felt."

Gina cared about Beth, but she also needed to honor her limits by listening to the cues her body was sending. Gina was discovering her *window of tolerance*, a term coined by psychiatrist Dan Siegel that describes a window "within which an individual can function well."[8] Trauma therapist Aundi Kolber defined the window of tolerance in her beautiful book, *Try Softer*, as "the range in which we can experience emotions, sensations, and experiences without feeling physiologically overwhelmed."[9] As Gina paid attention to signals that her body was overwhelmed, she started to make wise decisions on behalf of herself.

Becoming aware of your window of tolerance in various situations helps you find your voice. When you notice that ping of anxiety—your heart starts to race, your palms sweat, or you feel tense inside—pay attention. That's your body giving you an important cue. It might be that you are unsafe. Or it might be a sign that you need to say no, or at least, "Not now" to what's in front of you in order to honor your own limits.

Get curious about the reactions of your body and pay attention to the cues. You don't have to act on everything your body tells you. But as you learn to listen to her, your body will guide you toward the best of you.

Living From Within

Finding your voice isn't a one-and-done endeavor; it's a practice, a whole new way of being. It's learning to honor the contents of your soul and body—in partnership with God's Spirit—so your voice flows from a connected, authentic place deep inside. As you fine-tune the instrument God has given you, you'll be surprised at the voice coming out of you—a voice that increasingly knows what to say and how to say it when you least expect it. This voice moves from deep within the sacred *I* into the world around you. It says

- "I am here."
- "I have a perspective that matters."
- "I have something to say."
- "I want you to hear me. But even if you don't, my voice is here to stay."

It's the place where the truth of what you're experiencing comes together with the truth of who God is. The place where your "I feel" or "I think" comes together with God's "I AM."[10]

This is a strong place deep inside from which you begin to shape the world around you. Instead of reacting or responding, you start to show up authentically. You're connected. You're real. You're living out loud. You live out of a confidence that knows deep within that *no one can take my place in this world.*

You're no longer concerned with living *for* yourself. Instead you're living *from* the deepest, truest part of you.

Reflections

1. Find a picture of yourself as a young child. What do you feel toward that young child? If you notice anything other than curiosity or compassion, turn your attention to those feelings and get curious about them instead. Where do you think those other feelings came from?

2. Turn back to that picture of the younger you and reflect on how God sees her—as someone who is beautifully and wonderfully made.[11] What is it like to become aware of that younger version of you through the eyes of love, care, and compassion?

Chapter 6

But Won't They Be Mad?

The Secret to Setting Boundaries

I NEED TO GET SOME BOUNDARIES," LEAH SAID AS SHE entered my counseling office, tossing her long blond hair over her shoulder and swinging an odd-shaped bag on one arm. As she set the bag down to take off her coat, I noticed a tiny dog sitting calmly inside it.

The dog in a purse is something I've seen only a few times since, but the line she spoke is one I've heard hundreds, maybe thousands of times over my years working as a counselor. It's probably the most common reason women come to see me.

At this particular time, though, I was a brand-new counselor-in-training, completing my first year of internship. I soon discovered that my client, Leah, would become a teacher for me.

Initially, I took Leah at face value and set out to help her learn to say no to other people. But the truth is, Leah didn't seem to want to set boundaries. Instead, she wanted to come into my office each week and download all her frustrations about her friends, her boyfriend, and her family. Download, rinse, repeat. Week after week. No boundaries were being set and no progress was being made, despite my best efforts to honor her initial request.

At thirty-two years old, Leah had already been through a lot. She got caught up in a toxic relationship in her twenties, when she discovered her boyfriend had a secret drug addiction and was cheating on her regularly. He had become emotionally abusive, manipulating her every move to keep her from leaving him. Her parents helped her get out of that relationship by physically relocating her far away. Yet here she was in my office a few years later. She had a new job, a new boyfriend, a new set of friends . . . but all the same relationship patterns.

"Chuck is so self-focused," she complained at the start of our fourth session.

I already knew all about Chuck. He was Leah's new boyfriend. "He literally has no clue about all that's going on with me or the stress I deal with at my job," she said.

When Leah and Chuck first started dating, it was fire. She was the steady one while he was all charm and passion. He'd made her feel amazing—inviting her into a world of fascinating people and fun parties. But the sizzle of their initial flame had begun to dwindle. Chuck was starting to play hot and cold. One minute she was the most beautiful thing in the world to him. The next, he acted annoyed or angrily picked fights with her.

Leah tried everything she could to keep Chuck's attention. When he wanted her around, she was available. When he needed space, she gave it to him. She complained to me about their emotional rollercoaster ride during our counseling sessions. But despite the red flags I pointed out, she wouldn't exit the painful ride that Chuck was perpetuating.

After several weeks, it became clear to me that I was having *zero* success getting Leah to set any of the boundaries she'd initially said she needed. It came to a head when she found out Chuck had cheated on her in a drunken one-night stand. Rather than say no to his behavior, she said no to counseling sessions with me for a few weeks.

Eventually, Leah showed back up for another session. Sheepishly, she said, "You're going to fire me aren't you—for sticking with Chuck? My last counselor did."

This encounter with Leah led me to discover a hidden truth that I would take with me into my next two decades of counseling: Leah didn't actually want to set boundaries yet. A part of her knew she needed them. But other parts of her, deep down, had no intention of changing her relationship. I was going to have to get to know those other parts of her before we could resume talk about setting boundaries. So I started to get curious.

"I'm not going to fire you, Leah." I smiled. "I want you to keep coming to me, even when I'm concerned about the decisions you might be making. Here's the deal: I'll stop trying to get you to set boundaries with Chuck. But in return, I want to focus our time on *you*." From that point, Leah and I negotiated a new type of relationship. We'd leave Chuck off the table and instead start getting to know the different parts of her story.

Over the next few sessions together, I learned that she was frequently left alone as a child. Her parents traveled often, leaving her with random neighbors or babysitters she didn't know. She was taught that because she'd had her material needs met, she should never complain. As we dug deeper, it became clear that a part of Leah was desperate for connection. But Leah had learned to see herself as unworthy of it. The only type of love she understood was the kind she had to shove her own needs aside to get.

If Leah set boundaries with Chuck, she would jeopardize their connection. The young girl inside of her feared that lost, cut-off feeling she'd known all too well growing up. She was stuck between facing the loneliness of losing Chuck and the emotional roller coaster of staying with him. The roller coaster was winning. In order to be free, she first had to heal the loneliness of her past.

I learned something from Leah's story that has stuck with me to this day: Boundaries aren't primarily about saying no to other people. They're about saying yes to yourself and your own work of healing.

There is a reason so many women struggle to set healthy boundaries: the work of establishing boundaries requires a strong sense of self. It's extremely difficult to say no to someone else if no one ever taught you how to stand strong in your own power.

Furthermore, what do you do when someone starts using intimidating tactics or preys on your vulnerabilities? You've been taught to love others, to always be kind. Yet when were you last taught how to be discerning, shrewd, and brave? In particular, the Bible cautions us to be wary of "fools," "mockers," and "hardhearted" people who—due to their own unhealed pain—harm others. For example, when was the last time you heard the following messages?

- You don't want to squander your wonderful life, to waste your precious life, among the hardhearted (Proverbs 5:9).
- Escape quickly from the company of fools; they're a waste of your time, a waste of your words (Proverbs 14:7).
- "I am sending you out like sheep among wolves. Therefore be as shrewd as snakes and as innocent as doves" (Matthew 10:16).

The result? Setting boundaries poses unique challenges for women because we've been taught to deny ourselves sacrificially without a counterbalancing message.

The Yes Side of No

You might struggle with setting boundaries because you think the focus is on the other person. But it's not. Instead, redefine boundaries as saying yes to yourself and the holy work of healing. I call this starting with yes.

Imagine being so rooted in yourself that you simply do not tolerate a fool or a bully. You see their tricks a mile away, and you know how to stand firm in your power. With God's help, you are a force to be reckoned with.[1] Your boundaries are no longer focused on others. Instead, they flow from a strength you've built deep within.

This is what it looks like when you start with yes. Starting with yes strengthens your soul and establishes a support network. It clarifies your convictions and teaches you the skills you need to stand firm. It gives you a larger vision of the life you can claim so that when it's time to say no, you are ready.

As Leah and I continued working together, she said yes to healing the pain from her past. I asked Leah to describe what it was like when her parents left for a long trip. She told me how lonely she felt. A few times, when the loneliness felt particularly unbearable, she would break a glass bottle and cut herself with it. Something about the physical pain made her feel more alive, more connected. She never told anyone, and shame had seeped in.

When Leah told me this story, she connected to a painful wound that had been buried deep inside. As waves of loneliness flowed out of this tender part of her, we both grew quiet out of respect. Leah and I stayed present with the emotions she was finally experiencing, emotions that had been trapped inside layers of hard-earned survival.

In the presence of a compassionate witness, the trauma of her neglect came out from where it had been locked up inside her soul. This part of her deep inside still carried the weight of a burden she had picked up: *You're not special enough for them to stay.*

Leah and I didn't have any conversations about Chuck or about boundaries during that session. Yet something powerful had happened inside her. As the loneliness of her childhood was given a voice, she felt tremendous compassion for her own experience. She gained a glimpse of safety, belonging, and connection. As a result, she grew stronger inside.

There was one more hurdle to cross, however, before Leah was ready to fully commit to the yes she wanted to say to her future. She had to reckon with empathy.

The Empathy Trap

Empathy is the ability to *feel with* another person. It's not feeling sorry *for* them. It's stepping inside their perspective and experiencing it as they do. If you are empathetic, you hold a powerful and precious gift. When you understand someone's pain, they feel seen. Empathy drives out shame. It brings connection into desolate places. Empathy is the oxygen of healing.

But if you've been wounded, especially as a child, your "empathy meter" can get knocked out of whack. For example, empathy allows you to understand the pain behind someone's harmful behavior—even when that behavior hurts you. You may sense their shame, making it incredibly difficult to confront them. Your empathy may lead you to let someone off the hook when what they actually need is accountability.

If you are an empathetic person, one of the most difficult realities you will have to face is the reality that sometimes people can be small, petty, manipulative, or downright cruel. Even the people you love.

This is the peril of misguided empathy. It's like a trap. And it had ensnared Leah.

"Leah, I know we agreed not to talk about Chuck, but I can't help but wonder, why are you staying with him?" I attempted to wade in gently during one session.

Leah thought about it for a moment and then replied, "I know how much he struggles. I want to help him. Despite the way he treats me, I understand his pain."

Leah's empathy made sense. She'd been so hurt by her parents' rejection that she had made a promise to herself: *I'll never hurt someone else the way that I felt hurt.* I didn't want her to stop caring about other people. But I didn't want her to care about others while causing injury to herself. So we began to discuss the way out of the empathy trap.

It starts with courage. Courage gives you the mental and spiritual strength to name what is wrong and to stand for what is right. Think about it. Folks who lack empathy don't need a lot of courage to use their voice. They aren't aware of (or don't care about) how others feel. So, they simply steamroll over them. But that's not you. You *do* care about what they feel. You can't just move on, at least not that easily. If you're an empathetic person, you must develop courage to create the change that you need.

Empathy tells you, *Do not hurt anyone no matter what.* Courage takes empathy by the hand and gently redirects her, saying, *I see you. You are so deeply feeling. But I need you to trust me on this. It's not OK to let someone else mistreat you, just because you understand the hurt behind their behavior.*

Courage breaks silent pacts that are hurting you.

Courage seeks help outside of a broken system.

Courage speaks up on behalf of wrongs that you see.

Courage protects you, or someone you love, from mistreatment.

Courage brings wise leadership to empathy.

You can have empathy for someone and still hold them accountable for behavior that hurts. You can have empathy for the pain behind someone's harmful actions and still refuse to put yourself in harm's way. You might understand that someone doesn't mean to hurt you, while acknowledging to yourself that they are, in fact, causing you pain. You are not always called to *act* out of the empathy you feel, especially when you're the one who has been hurt. Instead, *notice* the empathy you feel and pause before you take action.

> **You can have empathy for someone and still hold them accountable for behavior that hurts.**

It's one of the toughest skills to learn as an empathetic person—especially when the one causing harm is a parent, child, spouse, or someone important to you. But you must steward your empathy wisely, with courage. You get to choose when you extend it and when you reel it in to protect yourself.

The Spectrum of Toxicity

"What do I do now?" Leah asked me several months into our work together. "I know Chuck isn't treating me right. And he's not changing. He just turns it on me, making me feel like I'm the one causing problems."

Break up with him! a voice inside of me screamed. Instead, I took a deep breath and considered my response. Chuck was showing his true colors, which I knew would eventually happen. He wasn't apologizing or trying to change. He wasn't showing any effort to become a better partner for Leah. Instead, he was using toxic strategies to keep her from leaving him.

So, I taught Leah about the spectrum of toxicity.

As you consider your own relationships, recognize that healthy behavior and toxicity exist on a spectrum. Very few people are totally toxic, and no one is entirely healthy.

This means that expressing your voice requires nuance and dexterity. You don't want to come down with a hammer when a flyswatter is needed. You also don't want to let someone who is using toxic strategies twist your best efforts.

There's no one-size-fits-all response when it comes to using your voice in your relationships. As you consider the many ways to respond to others, consider the example of Jesus.

Jesus navigated through complex relationships with unbelievable skill. Sometimes he left people in order to nourish his own soul. Sometimes he headed straight into hard conversations. Jesus was full

GASLIGHTING

- "I didn't borrow your phone. Why are you always blaming me?" (In fact, they did borrow the phone.)
- "I'm not drinking! You have trust issues." (In fact, they have started drinking again.)
- "I never said those things. You must have misheard me." (In fact, they did say those things.)
- "I'm not mistreating you. You have an issue with authority. You need to pray and ask God to change your heart." (In fact, they are mistreating you.)

MANIPULATION/GUILT-TRIPPING

- "You don't *really* care about me."
- "I know how busy you are; I guess you don't have time for me."
- "If you really loved me, you'd . . ."
- "If you really loved God, you'd . . ."

CONTROLLING

- "I forbid you to see that therapist/friend/family member anymore."
- "If you break up with me, I'll tell everyone who you really are."
- "You can't survive without me. I own the finances."
- "God has given me authority over you."

Make no mistake, these are big red warning lights. You can't change the other person. So, you must learn to protect yourself. When it comes to toxic behaviors—words won't work. With toxic behaviors, every word you say is going to get stuck in a web of confusion. In these cases, actions speak louder than words ever will.

How to Communicate a Boundary

When you deal with healthy people on the right side of the spectrum, use the following steps to speak up about your need to establish a new boundary line.

1. Prepare. Fewer words are clearer.
2. Affirm the good.
3. Tell the truth—don't make up excuses.
4. Start with yes. Name the yes you are saying that requires the no.
5. State the boundary line.

Start by practicing with people who have proven to be trustworthy. Script out what you want to say using the steps above to guide you. Here's an example:

I'm so grateful for your friendship. I'm saving money, so I'm not going to eat out as often. But staying connected to you is important to me. I'd love to plan a time to take a walk together each week. Would you be up for that?

It can feel uncomfortable to establish new boundary lines, even with dear friends. Some people won't like it. The truth is that the people who love you will understand. The ones who don't won't be able to tolerate the change. Either way, it's better to know than to continue to expend unnecessary energy.

Here are some sample scripts to use when you communicate a new boundary to someone who falls on the *healthy* side of the toxicity spectrum.

- **Needy Friend or Family Member:** "I know you have a lot on your plate, and I'm glad you trust me to reach out for help. I need to limit my phone use right now. But I'd be happy to schedule a regular time to check in. Let's look at our calendars."
- **Leaving a Group:** "I'm grateful for this community and what we've learned together. But I need support that is more specific to my season of life. So I won't be participating in the group anymore. I hope to stay in touch in other ways."
- **Advice-Giving Spouse:** "I appreciate that you're trying to help me. But I need affirmation for what I'm doing right. I'm open for one constructive suggestion today. It would go down better if the advice came between two compliments. I love a good compliment sandwich!"

Remember: humor and playfulness are your friends, *especially* in healthy relationships.

Actions Speak Louder Than Words

When you must deal with toxic or abusive people on the left side of the spectrum, the most effective response is taking action, which speaks louder than words. You've likely already tried to have a conversation with the other person but nothing has changed. That channel is closed. Let me repeat: if you *could* have a constructive conversation with the other person, the relationship wouldn't be toxic.

This is what Leah finally realized about Chuck. For months, she tried to let him know that she could no longer tolerate his random bouts of silence. Chuck had a choice about how he responded to Leah. He could have met her with genuine effort, such as "I hear you, Leah. I'm struggling, but I want to change. I'm going to get the help that I need." He also could have backed up his claims with actions.

Sadly, Chuck didn't do either. Instead, he spewed every negative thing he could think of to make Leah question her own sanity. Leah finally broke up with him for good.

The hardest part about leaving a toxic relationship is that there is no closure or amicable goodbye in most cases. Your goal with a toxic person is not to get them to understand you. The goal is to take effective action to maintain your safety and sanity. Dealing with a toxic person is not about a tidy process of communication. It's about getting a safe outcome.

I know it's painful to realize. But with toxic behaviors, actions are necessary. You may need to script out your communication, but your action is what will work. Here are sample scripts to use with people who fall on the *toxic* side of the spectrum.

Critical Parent

> "I want you to enjoy the kids. But I'm not going to listen to your criticism of my parenting anymore. If you bring up my parenting again, I'll hang up the phone or leave the room. I'm happy to give you updates about what the kids are learning at school, but that's where the conversation ends."

In this case, you're saying yes to a relationship, but you're clearly defining its limits. If the person violates this boundary line, you'll need to back your words up with action. Don't make an excuse. Simply back up what you've already said. Consider these action steps:

- Leave the room when the toxic behavior or topics occur.
- Excuse yourself from the phone if an inappropriate topic comes up.
- Stop spending time alone with this person; use the buddy system.

Manipulative Friend

"I care about you, and I appreciate our shared history. But I'm not happy with some of the dynamics of our friendship, and communication isn't working. I'll be taking a few months away to get perspective."

Remember, if you could communicate constructively, you would. In this case, words haven't worked. The goal is to create healthy distance. Depending on the level of toxicity and the history of the relationship, you might need to write a letter or send an email. Or you may need to bring somebody with you when you communicate that you are taking time away from the relationship. Consider these additional actions:

- Stop responding to texts or calls.
- Don't engage in any attempt to talk about your relationship.
- Discuss only safe topics if you're required to be around the person.

If you bump into this person in other areas of your life, you can continue to be polite and civil. The key action is to not engage in any conversations about the relationship.

Substance-Abusing Spouse

"I care about you, and I'm committed to a healthy relationship. But I won't be around you when you're using. The next time you show up high, the kids and I will leave. If this situation happens a second time, I will move out until I see a plan and steps toward change."

If you're in a relationship with someone who is abusing substances or abusing you, please seek support as you consider these actions:[2]

- Leave the house if they show up high or become abusive.
- Move out of the house if need be.
- Call the police if you feel concerned about anyone's safety.

> **Setting boundaries doesn't mean you don't care about the other person. It simply means you've started caring more about you.**

If the other person protests, you don't owe them an explanation or a drawn-out conversation. You're not saying anything mean or cruel. It's okay to say nothing after you say no. Setting boundaries doesn't mean you don't care about the other person. It simply means you've started caring more about *you*. You're not trying to hurt them. You're doing what you need to do to take care of yourself. That makes all the difference.

Should I Turn the Other Cheek?

At this point in the discussion, many women will ask me, "But, shouldn't I turn the other cheek? Isn't that how we're supposed to deal with challenging people?"

Many people have been taught this phrase at some point in their lives. You might still hear it preached today. Some still teach that the best way to interact with a bully, a manipulator, or someone who is toxic is to turn the other cheek. Typically, we are taught that this means to

- look the other way, as if nothing terrible has happened, or
- offer ourselves up for more pain.

After all, isn't that what Jesus taught? Isn't that how he behaved?

Let's look at what the phrase "turn the other cheek" actually means. Here is what Jesus said:

③ • **Clarify the choice they are making.** For example, you might say
to your mother-in-law, "Your comment is critical of my opinion
and ignores what I asked. Is that what you intend to say?" (A
little attitude in your voice won't hurt anyone.)

Standing up for yourself is easier said than done. But it's important to see the strength in these examples. You're not asking for more
mistreatment. Instead, by turning the other cheek, you make it very
clear that you know exactly what is happening and exactly how you feel
about it. In some cases, it's helpful to think of that bully as if they were
a child. (They're acting like one!) This strategy can empower you not
to give their toxic behavior more attention than it deserves.

When Leah finally left Chuck, we sat in my office with her sadness.
She wasn't gloating; nor was she angry. She was brokenhearted that
he hadn't been willing to change. But she was also free. She'd gained
something far more important to her than a temporary hit of dopamine love. She'd gained her dignity.

She discovered the power of finally saying, "Yes, I am worth more."
It doesn't work to coddle a bully, nor does it work to yell, argue, or
defend. You likely won't make them understand. But you can turn the
other cheek, lift your head high, and meet them as an equal. In doing
so you draw a line in the sand that says, "You can try, but you can't
cross me."

Your Voice Is Here to Stay

After reading this chapter, I hope you understand the strength you
possess. You've grown braver. You can choose not to betray yourself
anymore. You no longer need to cloak yourself with invisibility or dim
your personality. You're starting to show up as your true self in your
relationships.

Sometimes others won't like it. It won't always be easy. You may second-guess yourself. Stick with it. Honoring your voice is a process that doesn't happen overnight. But you'll get stronger as you practice.

When you start to use your voice, you start to recognize the healthy people you actually want in your life. It's also freeing to others around you. When you stop enabling others, it can empower them to take responsibility for their own change. Your voice can inspire other people to get the help they need.

Are you going to get hurt and mess up? Sure; selfhood is a process, not a destination. But learning to become true is worth it, as you develop a sense of purpose and confidence from deep down inside that cannot be shaken.

Honoring your own voice goes hand in hand with the work of honoring God. As you refuse to betray yourself any longer, you honor the One who made you.

Reflections

1. Consider the spectrum of toxicity. Where does one of your challenging relationships fall?
2. In the context of that relationship, what is a yes you want to say to yourself or to your own healing?
3. What is a boundary you must set as a result?

PART 3

Express the Best of You

She no longer had the desire to bend herself into the frame of photographs where she was unwelcome.

Morgan Harper Nichols, *All Along You Were Blooming*

Chapter 7

What If My Parents Drive Me Crazy?

Healing Childhood Wounds

MY MOTHER IS MAKING ME CRAZY!" MIA EXCLAIMED, HER hands gesturing rapidly as she perched on the edge of my office chair, leaning forward with urgency. "I'm scared to have children. I couldn't stand it if a daughter of mine felt the way I do."

A bright woman, Mia was respected and well liked in her community. She was a beloved middle school teacher and had married a young contractor who was hardworking and honest. Her future seemed promising.

"My husband thought that by moving away from my mom it would get her out of my mind. But it hasn't. I don't see her that much anymore, yet it still feels like she's in my head. Every so often, she'll call me late at night and tell me how lonely she is. She's usually been drinking, and I try to get her off the phone. But I can't shake the terrible feeling inside. It's like I'm twelve years old again—desperate to help her but completely overwhelmed. It can take me days to recover. My husband doesn't know how to help, and I'm terrified I'm going to mess up my marriage."

"Mia, what was your family life like when you were twelve years old?" I asked, guessing that age was a key to her story.

"My dad left us and Mom started to spiral. I walked on eggshells around her. I never knew when she'd come down on me. Sure, she was nice to me in front of everyone else. But when we were alone at home . . ."

Mia's voice dropped off.

"What would happen, Mia?" I asked.

"It's not like she hit me or anything. It's just that everything was always about her. It's as if I didn't exist. In public, she'd brag about me to her friends and seem so wonderful. Everybody loved her. At home, though, it was totally different. She drank too much, for one thing. But even when she wasn't drinking, I never knew who would show up."

Mia continued, "Mostly, she would criticize me or point out my flaws. So I'd try to get the focus off me and rag on my dad or ask about her friends. I hated being alone with my mother. But I felt terrible for feeling that way."

Mia's mom demonstrated several signs of toxic parenting. Instead of growing up with a healthy sense of connectedness, Mia grew up feeling anxious and tense. She felt responsible for her mom yet she also resented her. Anger simmered constantly beneath the surface, peppered with a big dose of guilt. She couldn't figure out how to get unstuck so she could become the best version of herself.

Mending Old Wounds

Mia's experience is common for many women who were neglected emotionally, abused, or harmed by a parent. Even though she'd moved away from her mother and gained geographic distance, she hadn't yet mended her sense of self, claimed her own voice, and learned how to receive the care she didn't get as a child.

You might have a less obvious struggle with a parent than Mia's situation. Perhaps your caregivers were kind but distant. Or maybe they expected too much of you. Some parents may not appear outwardly abusive or act out of control. But they can still have a negative effect on your adult life.[1]

Healing from your past is often a multi-front endeavor. For instance, you have to name and grieve what was lost and engage in a process psychologists call *reparenting.* You're also addressing painful patterns in your current relationships. To complicate matters, you might be working through these new discoveries while raising children of your own. You'll likely question how you're parenting your own children, even as you try to heal the hurting child inside you.

Please be gentle with yourself. Parenting is a really hard job. The goal is not to become perfect. In fact, the goal of a parent is to be "good enough"—that's a real psychological term.[2] Your own healing is the best gift you can give to your children.

Remember that reclaiming your sense of self is a process. It's okay to be right where you are. Each small step that you take toward healing is a massive success by itself.

How Healthy Relationships with Parents Develop

Why was Mia still struggling with her mom, even years after she'd left home? I believe it's for one simple reason: we are hardwired to crave connection with our parents.

Most of us feel love and loyalty toward our family members, even when they've hurt us. We long to connect with our moms, dads, or caregivers even when circumstances out of our control make a healthy connection impossible.

It's a parent's responsibility to model healthy relationships in families.[3] Their job is twofold. First, parents help a child to develop a sense of selfhood. A key job of being a parent is to help children understand who they are. A parent holds the very first mirror up to help their child see themselves as God does. For example, parents help a child develop a strong sense of self when they

- teach them how to care for their body.
- help them identify what they are feeling or thinking about something.
- teach them how to identify and ask for what they need.
- help them establish healthy boundaries with others.
- help them respect a healthy no they might receive from another person.

Parents also teach their children how to separate from them. In essence, a parent's job is to equip their child to leave them someday.[4] This process of what psychologists call *individuation* varies in different cultures. Even when a child stays close to a parent geographically and emotionally, on some level they still need to lead their own lives.

In a healthy family, parents encourage their kids to individuate in countless, subtle ways. For example, children and teens express their growing selfhood when they make statements such as

- "I want to try things a different way from you, Mom."
- "I'd rather spend time with my friends this weekend."
- "I love you, Dad, but you're so embarrassing."
- "I'm not sure I agree with you about that issue."

If you felt safe enough to tell your mom or dad some of your true thoughts and feelings, you're lucky. Your parents created an environment in which you could assert yourself and become your own person. That's exactly as it should be.

On the other hand, if your parents undermined this process, moving into a strong sense of self can be extremely hard. Ironically, the more toxic your parents are, the harder it can be to separate from them in order to heal yourself.

When Parenting Patterns Turn Toxic

When you were young, you absorbed all sorts of ideas about who you were and who you could become. You didn't have the capacity to filter the good ones from the bad. Whether explicitly stated or demonstrated through action, these messages echo in your soul as you navigate your own life and make decisions about love, work, and family.

In homes with unhealthy parenting patterns, children receive these types of damaging messages:

- You're invisible.
- You exist to meet my needs.
- Don't be like those other people—do it the way I do it.
- It's selfish to have your own dreams apart from me.
- It's your fault that I'm behaving this way.
- You can't make it without me.

These toxic messages can be extremely hard to shake, wounding the core sense of self. You may struggle with feelings of guilt, a sense of worthlessness, chronic loneliness, or a fear of rejection. These feelings typically operate outside your conscious awareness. To cope, you might pick up strategies such as performing, perfecting, peacemaking, and people pleasing to get the love and sense of capability you crave. When that happens, it can be challenging to establish healthy relationships as you move toward adulthood.

The Six Harmful Parenting Patterns

There are six main parenting patterns that harm children: unpredictability, parentification, criticism, control, blame-shifting, and rescuing. Let's dive into each.

1. Unpredictability

A parent who struggles with mental illness, addiction, or who can't manage their own emotions creates an environment of unpredictability. A young child doesn't know how to make sense of a parent who is happy one day but can't get out of bed the next. It's not that a parent can't ever struggle. The issue is that a parent must help a child feel secure, even when the parent goes through challenges.

Mia's mom was unpredictable, which left Mia on high alert. Every day when she came home from school, her heart would beat rapidly as she put the key in the door to their apartment. Would Mom be happy? Would she be depressed or angry? Would she even be home? The unpredictability in her home kept Mia in a constant state of anxious activation. It wasn't only painful emotionally; her body also paid a price as stress chemicals coursed through her.

2. Parentification

Another harmful parenting pattern is *parentification*. This is a role reversal in which a parent relies on the child to care for *their* emotional needs. For example, your mom might have conditioned you to tell her what she wanted to hear. Instead of trying to help you understand your own ideas and perceptions about the world around you, she taught you to validate *her* feelings and opinions.[5]

Parentification can be extremely subtle, and most children don't realize its effects until well into adulthood. As a child, you don't know that it's not your primary job to validate or manage your parent's emotions. If you took on that role of parenting your parent, it can be extremely challenging to understand your own thoughts and feelings.

For example, when I first started asking Mia questions, she would often start by saying, "Well, my mom always says . . ." She only knew how to reflect her mom's perspective. Her ability to reflect the thoughts and feelings of others was uncanny. But she had very little ability to connect to her own feelings and formulate her own opinions. This disconnect made it difficult for her to develop authentic two-way relationships with other people.

3. Criticism

Criticism is a way of demeaning a child instead of helping her see both her tremendous potential and her growth areas. An overly critical parent damages your core sense of self by constantly pointing out your weaknesses and flaws. It leads to a deep reservoir of shame that takes time and attention to heal.

In Mia's case, her mother's criticism was rooted in her own unacknowledged shame. Mia's mom had grown up with an alcoholic father who was vicious to her when he drank. This was in an era when mental illness, trauma, and addictions weren't talked about openly. As a young woman, Mia's mom had no one to go to for help. So she drank—just as her dad had done—as a way to mask the pain. Shame didn't go away. Instead, it festered in hidden corners of her soul.

When Mia's mom felt vulnerable or threatened, shame would roar up out of these hidden places. She'd offload it onto Mia, saying things like, "You're not so perfect, yourself. Do you think you're better than me?" She would also berate Mia for being selfish or ungrateful.

Unknowingly, her mom passed on a legacy of shame to Mia. On

one level, Mia knew her mother had been shaming and critical because of her own wounds, but young parts of her still wondered, *Is there something wrong with me? Am I selfish, like my mother says?*

Most humans pick up a strong shaming voice inside—an inner critic that points out everything you are doing wrong. It's hard enough to learn to manage this shaming inner critic without a parent adding ammunition to it.

Children need to learn that they are precious, valuable, and have intrinsic worth in order to grow a healthy sense of self. When you're exposed to constant criticism, whether it's a thousand subtle comments or the screaming vitriol of verbal abuse, shame's voice gets loud, eroding a core sense of your fundamental worth.

4. Control

An overly controlling parent undermines a child's need for autonomy. Control can take many different forms. It might look like possessiveness, in which the parent tries to stop a child from growing close to other people. A controlling parent might dictate a child's friends, interests, or choices, instead of teaching her to grow in wisdom and discernment. Or they may hold rigid "family dogmas" that stifle curiosity, creativity, and play. Here are some examples of how control might show up in spoken or unspoken messages:

- "Why would you want to XYZ?"
- "Our family does not do _____."
- "You'd rather be with them than with me?"

Children cling to their parents early on, but over time they need to separate and explore who they are apart from them. When this process of separation is thwarted by a controlling parent, you don't develop a healthy sense of your own identity. You may see yourself only as an extension of your parents and struggle to claim your unique gifts, preferences, and capabilities.

5. Blame-Shifting

Instead of taking responsibility for their own behaviors, blame-shifting parents constantly shift the blame onto their child, another family member, or someone else. Children may doubt their own perceptions of reality, leading to a sense of helplessness and emotional distress.

Mia felt this keenly, as her mom often blamed her or her father for her drinking. It's one thing for a parent to acknowledge their challenging circumstances and their pain. That's not what Mia's mother did. Instead, she blamed everyone else for her problems.

In another example, I worked with a client whose mother also battled with addiction. While her mom's struggle was hard on the family, my client had much admiration for her mother. The mom took responsibility for her actions, never blaming others. She was transparent about her struggles and admitted when she made a mistake. As a result, my client had a strong understanding of personal responsibility. She gained confidence in her ability to own her own mistakes in the context of compassion. Children don't need perfect parents, but they do need to see their parents take responsibility for their actions.

6. Rescuing

Rescuing is when a parent doesn't allow natural opportunities for a child to learn resilience. As a result of their own anxiety or unhealed wounds, the parent overprotects and rescues a child from any form of pain. This pattern is more about the parent than it is about what's best for the child. Instead of teaching a child how to work through tough situations, a parent conditions her to see someone else as her source of rescue.

If you aren't equipped to face obstacles, it's difficult to move into the emotional maturity that adult relationships require. Instead of facing challenges with confidence and skill, you might tend toward a victim mentality, unrealistic expectations, or even entitlement,[6] a mindset in which you expect others to do your work for you.

This list of six harmful parenting patterns is not meant to lay blame. Many parents who engage in these behaviors are dealing with unresolved wounds within themselves. But the

Your parents didn't destroy you. They just created some roadblocks.

fact is that these toxic behaviors pass down wounds to children. Your parents may have provided you with food, shelter, clothing, and educational opportunities. But that doesn't mean they helped you develop a strong sense of self.

The good news is that you can heal from childhood wounds. Your parents didn't destroy you. They just created some roadblocks. You can uncover the beautiful God-bearing self that was lost, reclaim it, and learn to live from the best of you more authentically each day.

Six Steps to Heal from Childhood Wounds

The work of healing childhood wounds can feel daunting. But remember that taking small steps each day will get you miles fast. I've counseled hundreds of women who have reclaimed their lives one brave step at a time. You can do it too. As you do this work, you'll be better equipped to create healthy relationships in your life moving forward.

Step 1. Recover a Sense of Trust

If you didn't experience security growing up as a child, you may feel a sense of chaos internally. But you can teach yourself what safety feels like by building trust with yourself. Start by making—and keeping—small commitments to yourself each day. Choose something basic that also feels important to you. Make sure it's something you can follow through on and commit to it for one week.

Here are some ideas to help you get started:

- Wake up at the same time every day or go to bed at the same time every night.
- Read or pray at the same time each morning.
- Make your bed.
- Drink water.
- Journal for ten minutes each day.
- Move your body at a set time.

Be specific. For example, you might say, "This week, I'll take myself on a walk each day at lunchtime." Notice what it feels like to honor this commitment to yourself. As you finish out the week, decide if you want to keep the habit or discard it. Then decide on a new commitment. As you build consistency into your days and weeks, you start to trust yourself. You can do small things each day to create a sense of order and predictability, even when life feels hectic. You will also learn what types of rhythms work for you and what don't. Remind yourself that learning to honor yourself in small and big ways is key to reestablishing a sense of safety.

Step 2. Reclaim Your Worth

If you were criticized, abused, or ignored as a child, you probably developed some harsh self-talk in your mind. How do you change these harmful thought patterns? Start by observing—and shifting—your conditioned ways of thinking. Here are some examples to explain what I mean:

- **Notice critical self-talk.** Awareness is the first step toward change. Write down what you notice in a journal.
- **Extend compassion.** Believe it or not, the critical part of you has been trying to help. Instead of criticizing yourself for criticizing yourself, meet your inner critic with compassion.
- **Reframe critical thoughts.** After identifying critical messages, write down a statement that reframes that voice in a more constructive way. For instance:

- "You should be more like her" becomes "I want to be my best self."
- "If you were better, you'd be where he is" becomes "I'm not where I want to be yet. But each day, I'm going to do my best to take the next step."
- "You deserve this bad thing that's happened" becomes "I've made mistakes. And I'm also a beautiful soul made in God's image."
- "You'll never be as good as other people" becomes "No one can take my place."

- **Honor the tender part of you.** Visit a favorite spot, engage a fun activity, or let yourself take a nap. It doesn't matter what you do as long as you do it as a way to honor the part of you that's felt criticized in the past. If you notice a critical voice surface in your mind about these activities, meet it with a gentle reframe by responding:
  - "I'm committed to discovering what brings me joy."
  - "I want to delight in the way God delights in me."[7]
  - "My body is valuable. It's important for me to get rest."

Paying attention to the criticism in your mind helps you differentiate from it, creating space for the "inner voice of love" to emerge from God's Spirit deep inside.[8]

Step 3. Recover Your Identity

If your parents didn't help you explore your own interests, opinions, and feelings, start with the basics of getting to know yourself better. Don't censor your response to try to come up with what sounds "cool" or what parts of you think you "should" feel. Instead, listen for the tender voice inside. Here are some questions to ask yourself:

- What kind of music do you like?
- What kind of food or restaurants do you prefer?

- Do you like to relax by working out or soaking in a hot tub?
- What makes you feel energetic and alive?
- Do you like your hair long or short?
- What hobbies sound fun to you?
- What topics do you enjoy discussing with others?

Give yourself permission to notice what you prefer, even if it's embarrassing or surprising at first. As you clarify your interests and preferences, notice how it feels to let yourself be you. Remember that what you like is a reflection of the unique way that God made you. Identifying your preferences empowers you to show up authentically with other people.

Step 4. Receive Care

If you were parentified as a child—that is, made to play the role of a parent—it can feel challenging to receive care from others. You were conditioned to meet the needs of others instead of learning to identify your own. But you can teach yourself how to ask for the care you need.

You might start by seeking out a one-way relationship with a counselor, mentor, or spiritual director in which someone is trained to care for you. Remember Mia's story? The first thing she did was find a counselor to provide her with the support she'd never received. Whatever source you choose, be clear about asking for what you need: someone who will hold up a mirror of truth to help you understand yourself.

Receiving care also means learning to ask for help in two-way relationships. Asking for help from friends or loved ones is a muscle you might not have developed. You might feel guilty, anxious, or even skeptical at first. Practice by taking small steps. For example, you might ask a friend for a ride or answer honestly when someone asks how your day is. Think of the easiest request you can make, and challenge yourself to reach out at least once a week.

Don't be deterred if it doesn't go well. Sometimes people will let you down. But as you develop your asking-for-help muscle, you'll discover the people who will show up for you.

Step 5. Reclaim Your Voice

If your parents didn't teach you how to express yourself in a healthy way, it's easy to get lost in the strongest voice around you. How do you reclaim your voice and learn to assert yourself? Here are several ways to begin the process:

- **Practice voicing your opinions with a safe person.** Start with a trusted friend, counselor, or family member. You might say, "I'm working on understanding what I think. Would you be willing to listen while I process my thoughts on XYZ?"
- **Assert your preferences in small ways.** Instead of agreeing to meet your friends on their side of town or at a place they recommend, practice suggesting where you'd like to meet instead. For instance, you might say, "What if we met at this coffee shop near me?" or "I'd love to see this movie. Are you open to that?"
- **Insert more of what you think into conversations.** Expressing your preferences doesn't mean you have to pick a fight. But practice speaking honestly, even as you honor another's perspective. For example, you might say:
    - "That's not something I struggle with, but I appreciate learning more about you."
    - "I understand where you're coming from, but I see that situation differently."
    - "I appreciate you sharing. I need some time to think about my opinion on the matter."
    - "Are you open to hearing my perspective?"
- **Take a class to develop confidence in a new skill.** Try a class that requires expressing yourself, such as acting, writing, drawing, dance, public speaking, voice lessons, or self-defense. Sign up for

something that appeals to you and teaches you how to use your body and mind in expressive ways.

- **Join a support group through your local community.** Support groups, such as Celebrate Recovery, Alcoholics Anonymous, and Al-Anon, are safe places where you can speak honestly without judgment. These options can be a great place to practice discovering how to use your voice.

Each small step helps you develop tolerance for uncomfortable feelings that surface when you tell someone what you feel or need. When you express your voice in small ways, it equips you to advocate for yourself in bigger ways.

Step 6. Protect Yourself from Further Harm

As you take steps to heal your sense of self, it's crucial to protect this sacred space. Some people won't appreciate the changes you make. Here's an example of how Mia established healthy boundaries to protect herself.

As Mia laid out a plan for reclaiming her sense of self, she started to get excited. For the first time, she felt hope she might be able to heal from the past and grow into a confident, purposeful woman. But Mia also knew how vulnerable she was to the late-night phone calls from her mom. And she was more motivated than ever to protect the commitment she'd made to herself to heal. Here's what happened next. With the support of her husband, Matt, she wrote a letter to her mom:

Dear Mom,

I love you, but I will no longer talk to you when you've been drinking. As a result, I will no longer receive telephone calls from you. In addition, I need several months to work on myself. So I won't be available by email or any other form of communication during that time.

If you have a health emergency, you can email Matt. Otherwise, please don't contact either of us until I reach back out.

I hope you'll seek out the help that you need. There is an AA program in town, and I know people who would be happy to take you to their meetings. But it's your job to figure out how to get the help you need.

Mia

Next, Mia blocked her mom's phone number and email address.

After sending the letter, Mia felt waves of emotions for several days. She anticipated her mom's emotional backlash: the shock, the anger, the sadness. She envisioned her mom frantically calling friends to say, "Can you believe what Mia did?!" She imagined the ways her mom would spin the story to make herself look good: "Poor thing. Mia must be losing her mind."

But Mia was fortified by the important work that was in front of her—the work of saying yes to healing herself and becoming a whole person. The emotions from sending the letter passed, and Mia stayed focused on the commitments she'd made to herself. She knew she couldn't heal while she was ingesting her mom's poison. Mia also knew that continuing to enable her mom wouldn't solve anything.

To be clear: Mia didn't establish boundaries to hurt her mom or to retaliate. She didn't set them because she was bitter or because she was avoiding a hard conversation. Instead, Mia set these boundaries because she had absolute clarity about what she needed in order to say yes to healing herself. The goodness of that yes made the difficult no feel grounded—even holy.

Mia spent the next several months making good on the commitment she'd made to herself. She sought guidance through weekly counseling and took tiny steps each day to grow in connectedness and authenticity. Some days were hard, and sometimes she still felt sadness or anger. But she stayed committed to herself and grew stronger.

After several months, Mia reconnected with her mom. Her mom

never apologized and never acknowledged her drinking problem. But she never again called Mia when she was drunk. In many ways, Mia's mom didn't change.

In contrast, Mia changed significantly. She became more of who she really was deep down inside, more rooted in her core. As a result, she was no longer under her mom's power.

Not long after writing the letter to her mom, Mia showed up to my office with a big grin. "You know what I realized this week?" she asked me.

"What's that, Mia?"

"I love the life I'm creating. I'm so proud of myself."

And that right there is a counselor's dream session. Mia was discovering her true self and the power of claiming her own life.

You may not wish to sever ties with a parent. Mia knew her mom had support from friends, and Mia had the support of her husband. That may not be the case in your situation. Yet there are still things you can do to create space to heal. Here are a few things you might try:

- Limit communication to email. Respond to any phone calls or texts by email.
- Provide "fixed-schedule" attention. For example, send your parent an email or a letter once a month with news.
- Use the buddy system. Don't be alone with a toxic parent.
- Leave the room if a parent criticizes you or someone you love.
- Don't respond to manipulative or guilt-laden emails, phone calls, or texts.
- If necessary, you may need to sever ties altogether.

Toxic Parenting and the Bible

"Honor your father and your mother, so that you may live long in the land the LORD your God is giving you."[9] Many women I've counseled struggle with this biblical commandment that teaches us to honor our parents. It's an important concept worth noting, especially in the context of claiming your true self.

When women raise this verse to me as a concern, here are some of the questions I ask them. How would you answer these questions?

Does it honor your mother or father to

- enable your father's self-centeredness?
- damage your own marriage by staying fixated on your mom's problems?
- bend over backward to meet unhealthy demands?
- engage in conversations that almost always turn toxic?
- wear yourself out so you don't have energy for your own work, spouse, or children?

I don't believe "honoring your father and mother" is represented by the situations above. In fact, you might find that honoring a parent can feel very counterintuitive. It might have to do with empowering them to take responsibility. Notice the difference between empowering versus enabling in the chart below:

EMPOWERMENT	ENABLING
I believe in your ability to ask for what you need.	I'll do your work for you. I'll mind-read.
I'll tell you when you cross a boundary line with me.	I'll make you feel like what you've done is okay.
I'll be honest about what I see.	I'll make excuses for you.
I'll remove myself from toxic behavior.	I'll sacrifice myself for your toxic behavior.

In this light, let's flip the question about honoring your parents. For instance, does it honor a parent to

- remove yourself from inappropriate, harmful behavior?
- heal your wounds so you don't pass them down to your children?
- create healthy distance but harbor a posture of forgiveness in your heart?

It's time to say yes to empowerment and no to enabling others.

A New Life Ahead of You

I know that the topics covered in this chapter may not be easy to digest, and some points could be misconstrued. Please know that these words are never meant to grant a license to cut people off with cruelty, especially a family member. But if you've been harmed or abused by a parent, I want you to know that prioritizing your own healing is not selfish. It's the first step toward breaking the bonds of generational trauma.

Here is what I know to be true:

- You are worth more than being somebody's doormat.
- You are worth more than being tossed aside.
- You are worth more than the crumbs that were given to you.
- You are worth more than wasting your time on problems you didn't create.

Prioritizing your own healing is not selfish.

- You are worth more than hating your body because your parents criticized or abused you.
- You are worth more than losing your sanity—and your potential—because someone else wouldn't get help.

You can heal. God wants you to become whole. He longs for you to unburden past hurts and say yes to a new life and the kind of healthy relationships he intended.

You can break free from painful patterns.

You can heal from your past.

You can claim the best of you that remains ahead.

Reflections

1. Consider the six steps to recover from toxic parenting. Which one resonates the most with you right now?
2. What is one commitment you can make to yourself this week?
3. Write out a plan for how you will honor that commitment to yourself.

Chapter 8

How Do I Find Friends Who Get Me?

Creating Authentic Connection

AS A COUNSELOR, I'VE LOST TRACK OF HOW MANY WOMEN I've met who feel lonely. Maybe you're experiencing that pain right now. It's difficult to go through life without having someone to share the ups and downs with. Maybe you've got some friends, but you wonder if those relationships could go deeper. Maybe you make friends easily but you still feel lonely, no matter how many people are around. Or maybe you've learned to keep people at a distance. You long for the kinds of friendships you hear other people talking about. But you can't figure out how to get them.

Take my client Tasha, for example.

"I have friends, I guess," Tasha said offhandedly during our first counseling appointment. "But I still feel lonely."

Tasha had come to see me because she was sick of feeling invisible, as if she was a sideshow in someone else's life.

Tasha paused for a moment and then opened up. "I mean, honestly, most of my friends drive me crazy. They're always talking about their problems or about things that don't interest me. They never ask about me. If I do mention something I'm worried about, they brush it off. I don't really like the events they're always hosting. I'm not on social media, and it seems like that's where they do most of their interacting. I feel like an oddball, like I don't fit in anywhere."

"I've heard you say a couple of things, Tasha," I reflected. "First, your friends look to you for support frequently but are not able to provide you with support. Is that right?"

"Yes, I guess so." Tasha nodded.

"Second, your friends enjoy big events and social media, and you don't enjoy those activities. Am I hearing you correctly?" I asked.

"Yes," Tasha said. "I mean, I try to fit in. But I don't enjoy myself. I feel bad, but if I say I'm not interested they get mad or hurt. So I just do what they want."

"So that's a third thing you've mentioned: when you state a limit or a preference, they get mad or hurt by that. Is that right?"

"Yes, that's exactly what happens," Tasha said thoughtfully. "I hadn't thought about it until now. I thought I was the problem."

"Tasha, I can tell you what's happening here," I said. "These aren't friendships. These are relationships you've created as a result of your conditioning."

Tasha arrived in my office with the idea that knowing women and being invited to events was the same thing as having friends. I assured her it wasn't. Over the next few weeks, Tasha and I began to unpack some of the conditioned beliefs she'd unwittingly picked up about friendships.

Managing Perceptions Versus Real Connection

Tasha had been taught to manage perceptions instead of forging real connections. She'd learned to gauge what other people wanted in order to earn their approval. But instead of feeling connected, she was plagued with a chronic sense of loneliness—of being an outsider looking in. She needed to move from managing how other people saw her to showing up as her true self.

Maybe you've picked up some misconceptions too. For example, do you relate to any of the following Seven P's of Managing Perceptions?

1. **Perfect:** If I appear perfect, no one can criticize me.
2. **Please:** I please others to earn love.
3. **Perform:** I make myself into what others want me to be.
4. **Produce:** I produce so they will think I have value.
5. **Peace-keep:** I stay small so no one can get angry with me.
6. **Protect:** I keep my guard up so no one can hurt me.
7. **Power-over:** I dominate. I take control of the narrative.

In Tasha's case, she believed it was her job to make herself into what others wanted her to be. She was introspective and curious about books, music, and history. But she had grown up in a family where her interests were criticized. Once, she brought home several books on wild animals, and her mom had exclaimed, "Oh, Tasha! Stop being a bookworm. How will you make friends if you keep your nose in a book?" Her parents pushed her toward an active social life.

When Tasha would enter a room full of people, her whole body deployed the conditioning she had learned since she was young. She told herself

- *You have to fit in.*
- *Set yourself aside.*
- *Figure out who everyone else wants you to be.*

How about you? What is your cloak of choice that you put on when you walk into a room full of people? Do you blend in so no one can criticize you? Or do you work to ensure everyone around you feels affirmed, encouraged, and cared for? Are you the workhorse who gets the job done? Or are you the entertainer who keeps everyone having fun?

Working to make the waters smooth for other people is not how you make good friends. It's how you become a wonderful houseguest.

There is nothing wrong with these qualities. In fact, all of them have their place. But if you *only* know how to manage perceptions, it presents a problem: working to make the waters smooth for other people is not how you make good friends. It's how you become a wonderful houseguest.

Instead, I want you to have friends who see the best of you and who stick around even when the worst of you shows up. I want you to have friends who help you chase shame away as they hold up the mirror of God's love. I want you to learn how to turn away from those who rob your joy and turn toward the people who bring you back to that tender, playful voice inside.

And to have friends like that—even just one friend at that level—you're going to need to know a lot more about relationships than how to manage other people's perceptions. When you work to manage the perceptions of others, you don't connect authentically from your core sense of self.

Managing perceptions means *I am trying to earn your approval through my actions.*

On the other hand, authentic connection means *I want to be known as I really am.*

Real connections develop as you engage these skills:

- Listening to the cues from inside your body.
- Expressing your voice honestly.
- Discerning who is trustworthy.

It's saying to others, "This is who I am. It's up to you to decide what you think about me."

But here's the conundrum: What if they don't like the real you?

This is the million-dollar question. Why do we work so hard to manage perceptions? Because a part of us believes that it's better to win approval than show up as we really are and risk shame or rejection.

If you stop managing other people's perceptions, they might not like it. They might judge you, get angry, or talk behind your back. In fact, my guess is somebody *will* do these things—and it hurts when that happens. But here's the real question to consider: Why work so hard to earn the approval of people who don't like the real you?

It makes no sense.

If you stop managing perceptions, you might discover

- someone will like that quirky aspect of your personality.
- someone will be thrilled to get to know your preferences.
- someone will see you—and love you—for who you really are.

They will. I promise you. I've seen it happen with numerous women I've counseled. And I've seen it in my own life. This is the outcome I want for you.

When you live from your true self, you open yourself up to wonderful possibilities when it comes to relationships. Instead of trying to win others' approval, you draw the right people toward you. Instead of cloaking yourself to fit in with expectations, you open yourself up to be known as you really are. And you are more available to show up in a healing, empowering way for others.

You also become less tolerant of unhealthy patterns in your friendships. Remember Tasha's experience? She spent time with several women; they just didn't happen to be friends. But instead of paying attention to what she felt about these relationships, she told herself the following self-defeating messages:

- *I'm terrible for feeling that way.*
- *I must be the problem.*
- *I'm just not lucky in the friend department.*

I want to teach you to do the opposite, like I taught Tasha. If you don't like something about a current or potential friendship, don't shove that feeling aside. Instead, get curious about it and measure it against the following red flags.

Seven Friendship Red Flags

It's hard to forge healthy friendships if your time and energy is spent on unhealthy situations. Here's how to tell if something is off.

1. Guilt-Driven Love

Do you stay connected to this person because you feel guilty if you don't? Are you afraid to say no to this friend because you worry that she won't be okay without you? For example, do you consistently overlook boundary violations because you feel empathy for her circumstances? There is a time and a way to wisely help others who are in need. But here's a tip from a therapist: A one-way relationship based *only* on helping the other person is not a friendship. It's therapy.

2. Fear-Based Love

If you set a healthy boundary, does the other person get angry with you? Do you avoid being honest about areas where you disagree? Maybe you fear the power this person has in your life or in shared communities. For example, do you fear that she might talk poorly about you with other people if you don't tell her what she wants to hear? You'll never become the best of you in a friendship based on fear.

3. Dopamine Love

Be wary of the initial "sizzle" in a friendship. Let me share some scientific research that explains what I mean. Stanford professor Robert Sapolsky provides a fascinating overview of how dopamine rewards the *anticipation* of pleasure.[1] Dopamine is a natural chemical that floods the mind and body with good feelings. Research on monkeys shows that when they learn to expect pleasure (food), their dopamine levels rise in anticipation of the reward. When the reward is distributed at *irregular* intervals, the level of anticipatory dopamine in the monkeys doubles!

What does this study teach us about relationships? We are conditioned to crave something that feels good or exciting. That makes sense. But what's fascinating is when someone bounces between making you feel amazing and then dropping off, it can *increase* your interest in them, leading you to crave something unhealthy. Pay attention to that initial excitement and proceed cautiously. Friendships must be tested over time.

4. Narcissistic Love

It can feel good at first to be singled out by someone who confides in you or leans on you for support. It's normal to feel good about yourself when you can help someone else. But what happens over time? Does she continue to talk only about herself? For example, does she get impatient or change the subject if you bring up something that is important in your life? Do you always meet on her terms? Are her preferences, activities, and needs always more important than yours? If your friend shows a pattern of being self-absorbed over time, pay attention to what she's telling you about herself.

5. Common-Enemy Love

Sometimes, friendships form by joining forces against someone else. Do your conversations revolve around a common enemy? In other words, is your friendship based on a mutual dislike for another person, group, or family member? Does this person spend most of her energy on being negative about other people? If so, you can bet it's only a matter of time before she is going to become negative toward you. Bonds are often formed when two people suffer similar pain, and there is nothing wrong with that. But if the basis for your connection doesn't move beyond a common enemy into building each other up, that's a red flag.

6. Controlling Love

Does your friend attempt to control your time, what you do, how you dress, or your other relationships? For example, do you conceal time spent with others from this friend because you don't want her to feel hurt? Is she jealous of personal time you give to an activity that doesn't include her? It's normal to be sensitive to each other's feelings, but ongoing possessiveness is a red flag.

7. Toxic Love

Some friendships can turn into abusive situations. Is this person cruel to you? Do they enjoy making you feel small? Do you worry that anything you share will be minimized, shamed, or twisted and used against you? Many women who grew up in abusive homes find themselves in abusive friendships. Toxic love is the only love you've known. If you notice this pattern in your relationships, please know there is so much more for you.

———

If you have a friendship characterized by any of these seven red-flag qualities, please take a closer look. It doesn't mean that you have to end the relationship immediately, but it's important to get clear about the unhealthy patterns that you see.

If you're in a relationship that has any of these red flags, ask yourself why you're staying in it. Consider the spectrum of toxicity discussed in chapter 6. Are you able to communicate about issues directly? If not, consider why you continue to invest time and energy into this person. Here are two key questions to ask yourself:

1. *What fears come up if I consider stepping away from this relationship?*
2. *Can I reduce my expectations in certain areas and still enjoy their good qualities?*

After reviewing the seven relationship red flags, you may realize that you don't have many healthy friendships. Facing this reality can be scary at first; it takes tremendous courage to recognize unhealthy patterns. That awareness may lead you into a period of adjustment and uncertainty. It's hard to disentangle from one kind of relationship when you don't yet know what a healthier one will look like. Transition can feel lonely, but that doesn't mean it's a bad place to be. Transition periods are an opportunity to learn more about what you desire and need out of friendship. This leads us to the healthy signs to look for.

Seven Signs of a Healthy Friendship

1. Respect

Do you respect this friend and how she lives her life? Respect is not the only ingredient of a healthy friendship, but it is an essential one. Are there aspects of her behavior or character that represent qualities you admire? You will become like the people you place around you. Therefore, it's crucial to develop friendships with people you respect.

2. Honesty

Does this person show that they want what's best for you, even if that means telling you what may be difficult for you to hear? This doesn't mean they criticize you about things that bother *them*. This means they care enough about your well-being to tell you when your beliefs or behaviors may be causing harm to yourself or other people. Likewise, does this friend value honesty from you? Do they invite your honest input and demonstrate respect for your viewpoint?

3. Reliability

Instead of the relationship red flag of "sizzle," look for consistent, measured patterns of behavior over time. Do you have a sense of how they will respond to you, even if they get busy? Would you call this person if you were in a crisis? No one is perfectly consistent. But a true friend shows predictable patterns of behavior over time.

4. Mutuality

Do you take turns sharing about various aspects of your lives? Do they know about your interests or struggles, just as you know about theirs? Do they show curiosity about what you think and feel? Does this person reach out to you? Or are you the only one who initiates? A healthy friendship flows two ways. You each know that you can count on the other person to show up for you.

5. Common Interests

Instead of a common enemy, healthy friendships share common interests. Do you share an interest in work, parenting, a desire to grow, or hobbies? Are you able to laugh together and enjoy rich topics of conversation? As C. S. Lewis said in his book *The Four Loves*, "Friendship must be about something, even if only an enthusiasm for dominoes or white mice."[2] According to Lewis, two friends don't primarily face each other as lovers do. Instead, friends are side by side, facing a common interest together.

6. Freedom

Healthy friendships aren't possessive or exclusive. Instead, good friends want what's best for you within the context of the friendship and outside of it. Healthy friendships don't *define* who you are. They *remind you* of who you are. Someone who has your best interests at heart can see you as a distinct person from themselves. They want you to thrive in every way, even if it means you expand your circles beyond them.

For example, is your friend happy for you when you discover other friends? Can she celebrate with you when you score a big win? That's not to say jealousy doesn't creep into even the healthiest of relationships. But when it does, can you both manage that in a healthy way?

> **Healthy friendships don't *define* who you are. They *remind you* of who you are.**

7. Emotional Safety

Can you share about your struggles without fearing judgment or shame? Not every friend will earn your deepest confidence, but a true friend nurtures a sense of safety. Does this person keep private what you confide in her? Do you trust her to hold what you share with care and respect? Emotionally safe people are comfortable with listening and seeking to understand before imparting their wisdom. They can sit with you in silence. They offer opinions without needing to be right. They offer advice without putting strings on whether you follow it. For example, when they do give advice, they say things like "Here's what I have found to be true" or "Here's what's been helpful to me" instead of "You shouldn't feel that way!"

Look through this list of qualities of a healthy relationship and think about your friends. Not every friendship has to meet every single one of these criteria to the same degree. For example, a friend you deeply respect may not be the one you turn to for a great time when you need to laugh. But a true friend will hit every one of these qualities on some level.

Here's the bottom line: the most important quality to look for in another person is compassionate self-awareness. When someone is self-aware, they are honest with themselves. They can reflect on their behavior, own up to it, and show meaningful steps toward growth. Self-aware people tend to be safe people. They are safe for others because they have found safety in themselves. Two self-aware people can forge a beautiful friendship that brings out the best in each other.

On the other hand, people who are not honest with themselves don't have the skill to be honest with you. Be cautious and wise about what you share with people who have not done their own work.

How to Find Healthy Friendships

Finding a good friend is a bit like the dating process. You might get to know a lot of people before you find those one or two individuals with whom you connect and who show themselves to be trustworthy over time. But if you commit to the process with care and intention, you will find new relationships that satisfy your needs and desires. As my mom used to say to me when I was struggling to make friends, "It only takes *one* to change everything."

"Hoping to get lucky" is not an effective strategy. Instead, start by taking an inventory of the key areas of your life. The more you lean into what you genuinely value and enjoy, the more you increase the likelihood of finding others who share those things in common. Here are four proven ways to start.

1. Shared Activities

Think about the hobbies you enjoy the most. It might be crafting or a physical activity such as jogging. Maybe you enjoy seeing the latest movies or talking about social issues. What are some ways you could pursue those interests in community?

As Tasha considered activities she might enjoy doing with a friend, she responded thoughtfully, "You know, I'd be happy if I never had to go to a big event or dinner party again. I'd love to find someone who wants to dig deep into a book or take a long walk." Armed with this simple awareness, she joined a book club at her local library.

It takes courage to put yourself out there, especially on your own. But by pursuing the activities you love, you increase the possibility of finding a kindred spirit.

2. Shared Faith

If your faith is important to you, consider asking someone to meet with you regularly to pray or read the Bible together. When I first moved to Boston as a single woman, I didn't know anyone. I nervously signed up for a spiritual retreat, where I got to know a woman who lived fairly close to me. We were both originally from the Rocky Mountains and connected over shared roots and a similar sense of humor.

She was a busy mom who worked in full-time ministry. When I raised the possibility of spending time together, she was candid about her limitations. "I don't have much time. But I'd love to pray with you on a regular basis." I respected her honesty and said yes to biweekly prayer meetings. That friend and I have prayed together twice a month for nine years. Yet we've almost never gone out socially. That's okay. We forged a relationship that met both of our needs, and as a result we know each other inside and out. Being clear about what you need and about your limitations creates a healthy foundation for authentic connection.

3. Shared Family Dynamics

Whether you're divorced, single, widowed, or married, look for a support group that caters to your unique set of circumstances. Then, when you first attend the group, get curious rather than rush in. Notice the kind of women who stand out to you, ones who say things that resonate. Consider asking someone to coffee to get to know her a little bit. If it goes well, try it again.

4. Shared Vocation

Notice the women you admire at work or who volunteer in your community. Maybe you respect the way they lead or share a common sense of calling. Don't underestimate the value of such relationships, even if they don't move outside of the work or service you do together. You might tell this person what you admire about her work and that you'd like to learn more. If things go well, add some structure. For example, you might suggest that you meet regularly to encourage each other in your work goals or service activities.

As you get to know potential friends, remember that trust is built over time. Proceed cautiously and keep in mind the list of seven relationship red flags. You don't want to get burned by moving too quickly. As trust develops, consider the idea that structure is your friend. As much as possible, get into regular rhythms with tried-and-true friends to ensure you're staying in touch. For example, you might set up a weekly walk or a biweekly meal together. Or you might set up a monthly Zoom call with friends who live far away.

No one friend will ever meet all your needs. You might find a friend you love walking with and another friend you love praying with. The important thing is that in each of these relationships, conversation is reciprocal and centered on encouraging each other to grow toward wholeness together.

Finally, if you're in transition and feel lonely, be gentle with yourself and resist the urge to rush the process. You'll be surprised how life-changing just one good friend can be and how one healthy relationship leads to more connections.

How to Test a New Relationship

Last, I want to address an important skill most women aren't taught: how to test a relationship. Testing doesn't mean putting the other person on trial. It's about showing *yourself* that you won't put up with less than what you deserve.

Remember when we talked about how identity precedes intimacy? You must be faithful to yourself, even as you seek to be faithful to other people. It's true for any type of relationship, including friendships. But as you've learned, women are conditioned to put others first, trust other people, and to stay loving and openhearted.

The truth is that your trust must be earned.

You can be kind *and* tough as nails.

You can be gracious *and* not suffer fools.

This idea of testing may go against everything you were taught. But it's biblical. Jesus told a number of parables related to the idea of testing. In one teaching he cautioned, "Do not give dogs what is sacred; do not throw your pearls to pigs. If you do, they may trample them under their feet, and turn and tear you to pieces."[3]

Likewise, the main theme of the book of Proverbs is to learn wisdom versus foolishness: "Whoever walks with the wise becomes wise, but the companion of fools will suffer harm."[4]

It's wise to be cautious when picking your friends. When faced with a possible new relationship, ask yourself, *Is this relationship worth my precious time, energy, and emotional bandwidth?*

This approach can feel uncomfortable at first, so I want to be clear: You can be polite to a lot of people. You don't have to give a lot of people the privilege of your friendship.

People tend to put their best foot forward at first. Therefore, it's wise to take it slow. Here are some ways to test a new relationship.

1. Practice setting boundaries early.

As you develop your voice, challenge yourself to introduce small boundaries early on. Remember, boundaries aren't about saying no. They're about saying yes to honoring yourself, even if it risks displeasing a potential new friend.

Why is this step important? It's your opportunity to build trust with yourself. You're no longer willing to please or perform for others at the expense of yourself. Here are some examples of what I mean:

- When you need to decline an invitation from someone you like, offer an authentic response, such as "I'm bummed I can't make it!"
- Share an honest opinion that goes against the grain.
- Pace yourself. For example, you might say, "I'm not up for a weekend getaway, but I'd love to meet up for a walk."

After you give your response, notice how they respond. Do they respect your no? Do they encourage you to share honestly about your opinion?

Or do they try to make you feel guilty? Do they get annoyed at you for disagreeing?

The way they respond is their choice.

In any relationship, you are responsible for

- being respectful in how you communicate,
- taking into account how your actions might affect others, and
- owning any mistakes you might make.

In contrast, you are not responsible for the way someone else responds when you disappoint them. In fact, how they respond provides helpful information. For example, some people will respect your actions. This builds trust. Others might distance themselves from you. Though this can hurt, resist the urge to control their response.

In some cases, people might even try to punish, pressure, or manipulate you. As Dr. Maya Angelou taught so powerfully, "When people show you who they are, believe them the first time."[5]

If a potential new friend reacts poorly, it's better to discover this red flag before you're neck-deep in a relationship. By setting boundaries early on, you communicate to someone, "I will respect you, and I will also respect myself." That's a great foundation for a healthy friendship.

2. Practice sharing vulnerability about small issues.

Everyone has vulnerable aspects of their story. You might feel tempted to hide those things. Or you might be tempted to bare your soul too fast. Neither extreme will help you build the trust you deserve. Instead, test the waters before sharing your deepest secrets.

For example, instead of telling your new friend every detail about your terrible relationship with your family, you might simply start off with "I wish I was closer with my family." Or instead of divulging all the details of your divorce, you might say, "I'm single now. I was once married."

Pacing yourself this way might feel foreign to you at first. But taking small steps with intention will help you discern who to trust. Remember, trust is earned over time. As you open up in small ways, notice how they respond.

- Do they push you for every detail before you are ready?
- Do they seem disinterested and quickly turn the conversation back to them?
- Do you feel criticized or judged?

These behaviors are red flags.

On the other hand, maybe your new friend listens and honors what you've shared. Perhaps, on another occasion, they remember what you said and are curious to learn more. By sharing slowly and strategically, you are communicating to this person, "I want to get to know you, and I want you to get to know me too."

3. Invite your new friend into situations and activities that matter to you.

If you are used to camouflaging yourself, it can feel uncomfortable to ask someone to do something you enjoy or to invite someone into a part of your world.

Years ago, I was yet again in the process of making new friends after having moved to a new city. One woman in particular caught my attention. She was smart, engaging, and hospitable, and she seemed to have a lot of friends and family nearby. I was flattered when she invited me to attend several events. She seemed to want to be my friend, and I was elated. But it soon dawned on me that I hadn't yet invited her into my world. I felt shy about my graduate school apartment and the quiet life I was leading, often alone with my books. I wondered if she would think less of me if I invited her into my sometimes lonely world. Mustering up my courage, I asked her to join me for coffee one afternoon.

She accepted my invitation and came over to my apartment. We spent hours talking about books, our mutual love of faith and psychology, and the loneliness we had both felt at various points in our lives. She told me about a model of therapy called Internal Family Systems.[6] That afternoon, a friendship was born that would become the seedbed for *Boundaries for Your Soul*, a book that I would eventually cowrite with this very woman, my friend Kimberly Miller.

New friendships don't always go that way. During that same season of transition, I joined a small group through my church. Within a few weeks, it became clear that this close-knit group of women wasn't interested in getting to know me, even though I kept trying to fit in. One day, the leader of the study sent out an email announcing options for a new time to meet. I decided to be honest about my limitations and told her the option that simply didn't work for me.

She picked the one time it was impossible for me to go, expressing no sympathy to me or interest in finding an alternative for my participation. The message was clear—I was out. Initially I beat myself up, thinking, *Why didn't I just tell them I'd be available at any time?* But then I reminded myself of the facts. As lonely as I was, I didn't want to be with people who didn't want to make space for someone new.

I moved on to look for other friends who were curious and open to making room for someone new. Making real friends can take perseverance but, I promise, you'll find them as you keep being you.

Creating Authentic Connections

We are all a mixture of wounded and healthy. If you assume that your job is to find the "good" people and put all your trust in them, you will quickly wind up disappointed. In addition, you will place your locus of control in the other person instead of doing the work of trusting your true self in partnership with God's Spirit.

Most relationships—even healthy ones—operate on a spectrum. There is joy and there is challenge. There is love and frustration. Your job isn't to look for a person to complete you. Instead, your job is to take steps to create authentic connections. Real connections form when you show up as your true self.

As you begin to risk expressing your true self, you'll discover the kind of people you enjoy—and who are also drawn to you. You'll gain confidence as you decide who you want to let into your life and why. This clarity becomes a superpower.

Together, you and a true friend will forge a relationship that breathes life into both of you. The results will magnify the good in other areas of your lives too. Finally, the more health you taste in friendship, the more your tolerance for toxicity will diminish.

Reflections

In his beautiful book *The Voices We Carry*, hospital chaplain J. S. Park described a profound exercise to help you discover what you need.[7] The following is an adaptation of his work.

To increase self-compassion, think of yourself in the third person. Now, consider the following questions:

- What qualities does [insert your name here] most need in a friend?
- What qualities does [insert your name here] bring to her friends?
- What steps does [insert your name here] need to take to discover the friendships she craves?

Chapter 9

Can I Get Someone to Change?

Drawing New Boundaries in Old Relationships

TIA PLOPPED DOWN ON MY COUCH AND PROMPTLY STARTED crying. "I'm so frustrated in my marriage," she said. "I don't know what to do. What I have is so much better than so many other people. I hate to complain. But it's so hard living with someone you feel like you barely know."

Tia went on to describe that her fifteen-year marriage wasn't terrible; nor was it great. Her husband wasn't abusive, but Tia said he could be distant.

"He completely tunes me out," she reported. "When I try to get him to talk to me, his eyes glaze over. It's as if I've asked him to do some terrible chore. We'll barely speak for a few days. But we eventually get back to the business of tackling the chore list together."

Tia wasn't happy in her marriage. But she wasn't unhappy enough to leave. Both she and her spouse were hardworking, responsible people. Yet slowly they had disconnected from themselves and from each other.

Tia's situation is common among many of the women I've counseled. The relationship isn't bad enough to leave, but it's not the true connection you crave. This type of frustration brings us to a question that confronts almost every long-term relationship: How do you create the change you desire?

Initially, most of us focus on the frustrating behaviors instead of identifying the deeper longing that we crave. But this approach is like fighting off each tiny pest that enters a flower garden. It's exhausting and not very effective. What works better is to identify what your garden needs to thrive, then set up regular maintenance that allows you to enjoy what's beautiful about it.

The same principle is true for relationships. You want certain behaviors to change, but, more important, you want a healthier, more vibrant connection. To achieve the latter, you have to identify what your relationship needs to flourish and create rhythms to support it.

Focusing on the problems doesn't work; nor does operating on autopilot, avoiding awkward conversations. Instead, you must learn to pay attention so that you can express your voice effectively. Above all, you must get curious about your deeper longing.

While you can't change the other person, you *might* be able to negotiate healthier boundary lines in your relationship if both people are willing.

When Needs Collide

It's normal to experience frustration with a partner, friend, or sibling. When we do, typically, we reach for one of two extremes. We either

1. lash out
2. ignore the issue and avoid conflict

Neither option works. The first option creates a lose-lose situation. You sound critical; they get defensive or fire back. You wind up in a toxic dance of angry exchanges. Even if you do get the behavior to change, the other person is not happy about it. And you haven't gotten what you actually desire, which is a stronger, healthier relationship.

The second option leads to long-term, chronic problems. Instead of addressing the issues within the relationship, many of us

- triangulate by venting to friends;
- numb legitimate concerns with food, substances, or entertainment; or
- shut down altogether.

These actions aren't healthy for you, and they further erode the intimacy of key relationships. Inevitably, the problems fester and come to the surface in bigger ways over time. So what is the solution? First, get curious about your own reactions.

An instinct to lash out or avoid typically stems from past wounds or conditioning. These reactions mask genuine desires and needs you may not be consciously aware of. The first step is to understand your own reactions with compassion. Start by getting to know the two main players in any potential conflict: criticism and guilt.

Criticism

Even in the best of relationships, needs don't always match up. Maybe you're an extrovert but your spouse has little interest in socializing with other people. Or maybe you crave quiet and simplicity, while your loved one constantly signs up for action-packed weekends.

These types of scenarios are normal in any relationship. But problems arise when you approach such differences with criticism. Here are some examples of how criticism expresses itself toward another person:

- "You're lazy."
- "You never listen to me."
- "It always has to be done your way."

These types of "you" statements almost always evoke a defensive response in the other person. They shut the conversation down instead of opening it up to the possibility of an honest dialogue. When criticism shows up, conflict turns toxic.

Maybe you don't *say* these things, but inside you think them. Unchecked criticism can lead to *contempt*, a disdainful view that renowned relationship expert Dr. John Gottman identified as the most destructive quality in relationships.[1] When you start down the road of criticizing your loved one, you hold up a broken mirror that reflects to them the worst of who they are, magnifying shame and eroding safety. It will not help you get the relationship you want.

Guilt

In addition to criticism, guilt can also keep you from addressing conflict constructively. While criticism points the finger at the other person, guilt turns it right back at you. Notice how guilt operates in the following examples:

WHAT YOU FEEL	WHAT GUILT SAYS
I feel frustrated.	You can't make him feel bad.
I am struggling with this.	How can you complain when others have it so much worse?
I crave time alone.	You can't disappoint them!

When you are guilt-tripping yourself, it's extremely difficult to acknowledge the genuineness of your deeper longing. On the other hand, if you can recognize conflicting feelings within yourself, you set yourself up for success.

When you notice criticism or guilt, start using what psychologists call *dialectical thinking*. Dialectical thinking involves two key components:

1. The ability to name two conflicting, but valid, feelings or ideas.
2. The capacity to honor both without judgment.

Here is what dialectical thinking looks like in the examples given above:

- "I feel frustrated—and—I don't want to be critical."
- "I am struggling right now—and—I want to be sensitive to the other person."
- "I need time alone—and—I don't want to disappoint anyone."

Do you see how each of these statements honors two competing facts without judgment?

When you can name competing feelings within yourself, it becomes easier to see a situation objectively. It also helps you to honor the competing feelings within someone else. For example, maybe they also feel torn between what they want and what they know you need. Instead of staying stuck between criticism and guilt, you start getting curious.

When criticism shows up, conflict turns toxic.

You can also apply dialectical thinking to the competing needs within your relationship. First imagine the best of you and the best of the other person. Now consider your colliding needs and state two things that are true side by side, without judgment. For example:

- I want to check in every day. She prefers a long conversation every few weeks.
- I want to do projects on the weekend. He wants to recreate.
- I value a discussion of feelings. He likes to stick to the facts.

As you identify legitimate differences, you'll gain compassion—for yourself and for the other person. Creativity kicks in and you'll start to discover new possibilities.

How to Draw New Boundary Lines

If you want lasting results, first get to the root of what really matters. Then you and your loved one can negotiate creative solutions together. Here are five steps to guide you.

1. See the big picture.

To go the distance, all relationships need a combination of autonomy and connection. If you've seen any movies that showcase old-fashioned dancing, such as *Little Women* or *Pride and Prejudice*, you've seen a great metaphor for healthy dependence. The couples move in a rhythm both toward and away from each other. They always stay connected, while interacting freely with others around them.

This metaphor captures the two foundational ingredients that we discussed in chapter 4, which are

1. autonomy: the space to be yourself
2. connection: a sense of togetherness with someone else

When two people err toward *autonomy*, they lose connection. This is what had happened in my client Tia's marriage. She and her spouse had begun living separate lives, and she longed for more togetherness. The boundary lines looked like this:

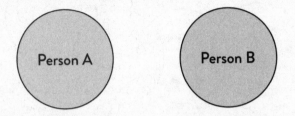

At the other extreme, one person can get consumed by the other. The relationship becomes codependent. If this describes your relationship, you might long for more space to be yourself. In this case, the boundary lines look like this:

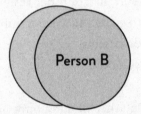

Despite what current self-help trends suggest, we do need to rely on one another. It's healthy to depend on other people. But we also need space to be our individual selves. Autonomy and togetherness are equally important. We need both to be healthy as friends, spouses, parents, or family members.

People are complicated. As a result, our needs and wants will never completely align. No relationship perfectly balances autonomy and togetherness. The goal is not perfection. Instead, the goal is harmony. With that in mind, here's an illustration of what healthy boundary lines look like:

In this diagram, you (Person A) and your loved one (Person B) share interests that overlap, and you remain connected to each other.

The overlapping area might include any number of shared interests and values:

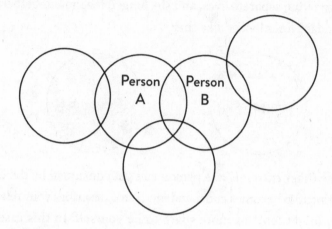

- Delight in your children
- Love of the outdoors, art, or other activities
- A commitment to goals you are pursuing
- Ideas you enjoy discussing
- Spiritual beliefs you hold

But you also have a sense of autonomy. You each have your own interests outside the overlapping area. You don't have to be on the same page about every single thing. Plus, you each enjoy other friendships, even as you share a few. There's connection and intimacy, yet there's space for individuality. Healthy relationships are characterized by the following:

- We maximize our strengths and focus on the things we share in common.
- We encourage each other to pursue our individual interests and talents.
- We don't agree on everything, but we respect our differences.
- We provide support for each other emotionally, spiritually, and physically.

The details of how this plays out will look different for every single relationship. For example, you might have a friend you talk to every single day. But you each also have other friends. Your loyalty is not exclusive. On the other hand, you might have a sibling with whom you share only a love for your children. Your overlapping circle is important but small.

Your marriage will look different from other marriages too. For example, one couple might pray together every night, while another couple might choose to pray separately. One couple might enjoy working together. Another couple might support each other in their different vocations. The goal isn't to achieve someone else's ideal. It's to determine what works best for your relationship.[2]

This big picture is your benchmark. It's a picture of what it looks like when both of you are thriving. It will also help you identify your deeper longing: *Do I need more connection? Or do I need more space to explore my autonomy?* When you see the big picture, you can focus on the major issues and put minor disagreements in a grace pile.

2. Get curious about behavior patterns over time.

Observing patterns in your relationship requires curiosity and patience. Instead of staying in the weeds of a hurtful moment, take a step back to look for trends over time. This process gives you perspective. For instance, you might ask yourself the following questions:

- When did he start tuning out through TV/alcohol/work?
- Was there a recent time when she asked about my needs?
- I wonder why he stopped helping around the house. When did he stop?
- Has she always been inconsistent about keeping in touch? If not, when did it start?

As you observe patterns, you shift from judgment and move toward curiosity. Remember, if you go into a conversation with criticism, you'll create a lose-lose situation. On the other hand, if you go in with curiosity and a big-picture perspective, you'll set yourself up for the possibility of success.

3. Identify the pattern's impact on you.

A *dynamic* is a pattern of relating that occurs between two people. The other person's behavior is one part of that dynamic. Your response to their behavior is the second part. It's often easier to focus on the other person. But the process of negotiating change requires you to get clear about how someone else's behavior affects you specifically. Start by creating "I" statements.[3] For instance:

- I feel frustrated when he disappears into the television.
- I feel abandoned when he defers parenting challenges to me.
- I feel anxious when she suddenly stops texting me.

In this step, you're still doing the work inside yourself. You're listening to the voice of your feelings and the tender one inside. You might realize that this simple act of naming your experience brings relief. Or you might decide that it's important to communicate about it. If you decide to communicate, you'll be prepared to express yourself with compassion and authenticity.

4. Clarify the deeper longing.

Next consider the following two questions:

1. What is the deeper longing underneath your frustration?
2. What could your relationship look like if you moved toward that longing together?

Again, start in the privacy of your own heart. Giving your loved one the benefit of the doubt, reframe the behavior in a noncritical way. Use the following sentences to guide you:

Start personally

I feel ▓▓▓▓▓▓▓▓▓▓▓▓▓▓▓▓ when ▓▓▓▓▓▓▓▓▓▓▓▓▓▓▓▓▓▓▓ .

I long for ▓▓▓▓▓▓▓▓▓▓▓▓▓▓ in our relationship.

Examples:

- I feel *frustrated* when *we don't check in about our evening plans*. I long for *more emotional connection* in our relationship.
- I feel *abandoned* when *we don't team up on parenting challenges*. I long *to share parenting decisions* in our relationship.
- I feel *anxious* when *we go weeks without talking*. I long for more *consistency* in our relationship.

Please don't move forward until you clarify exactly what you long for. It may feel vulnerable. You may feel like you're being demanding or burdening the other person. That's why it's so important to have done your own work first. Leading with the deeper longing takes the other person off the hot seat. Instead of trying to change details about them, it forces you to dig deeper into the good things you need and want in the relationship. The other person might not be able to meet this need, and that's okay. But you won't be able to have a healthy conversation about the possibilities if you don't take a risk.

5. Communicate.

After completing steps one through four, you're finally in a position to initiate a conversation.

Working out the details of a relationship is a bit like that old-fashioned dance. If you push too hard, you risk alienating the other person. If you don't speak up for yourself, you risk being a doormat. Expressing your voice is a process of learning how to articulate what you need without being rigid.

For example, when my husband, Joe, expressed concerns to me when we were still dating, he was communicating on behalf of what he needs in a relationship. He was saying, "I desire a relationship in which we discuss potential areas of conflict openly." He knew himself well enough to know that he'd feel frustrated if he was constantly trying to read my mind.

Rather than breaking us up, it launched an important negotiation between us about how we would communicate going forward.

A few weeks later, I returned to our previous conversation and said something like this: "I get that you value direct communication. I can work on that. Here's what I need in return. I need space to understand what I think and feel when we bump into a conflict. It might seem like I'm being withdrawn or distant during that time. But I simply need the time to understand what is actually happening inside me."

"And you need me to give you that space?" Joe asked to clarify.

"Yes. If you can give me some time and space to process internally, I'll be far more able to communicate honestly and directly with you. I can let you know by saying, 'Can I get back to you on this topic? I need some time in my turtle shell before I can communicate what I'm feeling.'"

"That makes sense," Joe said. "I understand."

In that negotiation between us, notice how several key things happened.

1. **We honored our legitimate differences.** When it comes to conflict, I tend to be avoidant, and Joe tends to want to get it out on the table. This difference could have gotten the best of us. Instead, we negotiated a way forward that worked for both of us.
2. **We labeled an ongoing dynamic that would help us stay connected.** When I identify that I'm going into a "turtle shell," we both know what is happening and feel a sense of togetherness in that situation. It brings us closer instead of driving us apart.

3. **We showed fidelity to ourselves and to each other.** Joe learned to honor my need for time to process internally. He has proven that he is trustworthy. In return, I use that time to get to the root of what I think so that I can communicate authentically. I earn his trust by following through on my commitment to circle back.

4. **We introduced playfulness into the dynamic.** "Turtle mode" (and countless other labels we've created over the years) helps us be playful with each other. We can laugh at ourselves. In any relationship, playfulness is a key component to staying healthy. If you can laugh together about areas where you differ, you're well on your way to health. Introducing creativity and play into your relationship helps keep the connection vital.

Whether you realize it or not, all relationships are negotiated. Healthy negotiation in relationships allows you to honor yourself while simultaneously honoring the needs and wants of the other person. It's the fruit of a strong sense of self, and it's a wonder to behold when you start to do it with care and intention.

In a romantic relationship, you typically negotiate important decisions such as where you will live, whether you want to have children, and whose parents will get you for the holidays. You also negotiated your relationship with your own parents as you became an adult. It might have been forceful if you clearly staked out new ground for yourself. Or it might have been subtle. Perhaps they laid out their expectations and you didn't know that you could have a say.

Friendships are negotiated as well. Early on, norms get established. Maybe a friend expected you to be available to them on a daily basis. Over time, you might find that you need to shift those expectations as a result of life circumstances. The good news is, your relationships can be renegotiated at any time.

The Negotiation Conversation

When you enter a conversation, here are some guidelines to help it go well.

1. Don't lead with your emotions.

Negotiating new boundary lines in any relationship works best when you are in charge of your emotions, not the other way around. As we explain in *Boundaries for Your Soul*, instead of speaking out of emotions, such has anger, first turn them into your allies by connecting to the best of you within.[4] Take the time to journal about overwhelming emotions or talk with a counselor or trusted friend. Get to know your emotions; don't shove them aside. When you express curiosity toward what you feel, emotions tend to soften.

Preparing yourself in this way reduces the risk of unruly emotions hijacking the conversation. Instead, your emotions will bring authority and authenticity to what you are saying. Even if the other person's emotions get hot, you can stay in command of yours.

2. Prepare what you want to say.

When you're new to this type of conversation, it can be helpful to write out a script. I often tell clients to pray about the conversation, then plan for it. Prayer will help ground you in the fruit of God's Spirit, such as patience, gentleness, and self-control.[5] Planning will help ensure that you don't default to your go-to survival response, such as fighting or fawning.

When preparing, use the following principles adapted from the ones you learned in chapter 6:

- Affirm the good.
- Start with yes. Name the deeper longing.
- Propose an option that might work for you both.
- Stay curious, brave, and compassionate.

In the situations below, which of the following communication options do you think would go over better with your loved one, assuming they are on the healthy side of the spectrum of toxicity?

Option 1: "I hate it when you disappear into the TV!"
Option 2: "I love spending time with you. And I feel frustrated when we don't check in about evening plans. Would you be open to talking about some activities we could enjoy together?"

Option 1: "You never help me!"
Option 2: "I appreciate your trust in my parenting. I've noticed that as the kids get older, I'm longing to wade through these challenges together. Are you open to setting up a weekly time to check in about parenting decisions?"

Option 1: [Suffer in silence, while saying nothing.]
Option 2: "I'm so grateful for our friendship. And I know you have a lot on your plate. I'm realizing how anxious I feel when I don't hear from you for long stretches. Could we talk about a communication rhythm that works for both of us?"

Speaking up for yourself is a risk, but what do you have to lose? You might be able to negotiate real change in your relationship. And if the other person can't meet you halfway, it's important to find that out so that you can get your needs met in other ways.

Learning to express your voice is a process. You may need to work up the courage to speak up in this way. You might enlist the help of a friend, mentor, or counselor. No matter how long it takes, the principles still stand. If you can learn to see the big picture and ask for the changes you desire, you'll start experiencing the kind of relationships you want.

What If Negotiation Isn't Possible?

Negotiation works only when both people involved are open and willing to make changes. If your loved one is engaging any of the following behaviors, negotiation will not work:

- Blaming you for their behavior.
- Verbally berating or physically harming you.
- Twisting the truth to make you feel crazy (gaslighting).

This person is using tactics designed to shut you down or control you. In these cases, normal communication strategies won't work. Instead, you will need to claim your voice with action.

Remember: when it comes to toxic behaviors, actions speak louder than words.

Grow Anyway

As you heal, your relationships will change. Your loved one might not understand the changes you desire, especially at first. They might feel threatened or fearful. Growth will shake things up. Some relationships will rise to meet that challenge. They'll make the adjustment with you. Some won't. *Grow anyway.*

Start by using your voice in your safest relationships. Look for small wins first. You don't want to take big swings right out of the gate. When you're ready, take one brave step at a time. This is exactly what Tia had to do in her relationship with her husband in order to create the connection she craved.

She started out with small requests:

- "Could you sit next to me when we watch a movie? I'd love it if you held my hand."

- "I need you to show interest when I tell you about what I'm learning in class. This is important to me. It matters."

In Tia's case, her husband was also inspired to grow. Instead of blaming Tia for his distance, he started working on healing his own wounds. As each of them focused on the work of becoming more of their best selves, they began to negotiate a healthier, more satisfying marriage. Instead of blaming or avoiding each other, they learned to speak up honestly on behalf of deeper longings. When they didn't agree, they learned to negotiate and play.

Not every relationship works out this way. I've worked with other women who started to heal only to find their loved ones grow even more distant or angry. It's painful.

But think of it this way: Would you rather continue to betray yourself? Or do you want to become the best of you, regardless of the choices other people make?

This process takes time, but it will lead you to better results in the long run. It will help you pick the battles that are essential for a successful relationship. You'll learn to set aside the ones that don't really matter. Best of all, you'll approach these conversations with clarity and confidence. Regardless of the outcome, you'll have the satisfaction of knowing you showed up as the best version of yourself.

Reflections

1. When you're frustrated in a relationship, do you tend to blame others (criticism) or blame yourself (guilt)?
2. What comes up for you as you consider the deeper longing that you have for your relationship?
3. Is there one relationship in particular where God might be nudging you to speak up for yourself in new ways?

Chapter 10

Why Doesn't God Just Fix Everything?

Healing Your Relationship with God

THROUGHOUT THIS BOOK, WE'VE EXAMINED LIFE IN THE context of various relationships, such as your parents, friends, or spouse. But there is another relationship that is more important than any of the people we encounter.

As I write this chapter, I am keenly aware of stepping on holy ground. Healing our relationship with God is the most important work we do to become our true self.

You are a beautiful soul made in God's image, cherished by the One who made you. Yet, in my experience as a counselor, I see the devastating effects of childhood wounds and toxic messages on this precious relationship all too often. Working to heal that relationship is the most rewarding—and most humbling—part of my work. I see damaged relationships with God show up in two specific ways.

First, I see the effect of spiritual abuse. The name of God or various spiritual practices have been misused in a damaging way, which creates harm to a soul and a distorted view or distanced connection with God.

Second, I see the effects of the cocktail of codependency, which includes the childhood wounds, confusing church messages, and cultural conditioning that we have discussed in the context of other relationships. Unknowingly, a relationship with God takes on some of these codependent features, keeping a soul from the kind of loving partnership God wants.

In this chapter I want to address both spiritual wounds and spiritual codependency in two distinct sections. My goal is to set you on a path toward healing if you're experiencing either of these tendencies.

A Story of Spiritual Abuse

Rue was magnificent—a unicorn of sorts. Over six feet tall, with dark hair cascading over strong shoulders, she was engaging, charismatic, and smart. A towering giant on the basketball court, she was also an emotional and spiritual orphan.

When Rue came to see me, she was newly married and experiencing signs of trauma, especially when she went to church. Her situation posed a problem not only because it hampered her spiritual life but also because her husband was a pastor. It was hard to explain to the congregation that his wife couldn't attend church on Sundays because listening to someone read from Scripture or talk about God gave her a panic attack.

Rue's body was speaking loudly to her, despite her best efforts to silence it.

As I got to know Rue's story, I discovered how prayer, the Bible, and even church attendance had been turned into weapons and used against her. The abuse culminated when Rue's parents kicked her out of their house when she refused to apologize for texting with a boy from church. She was seventeen at the time, but the real problem had started long before that incident. The truth was, Rue had been working overtime to please her father for years.

As we unpacked her story, Rue explained that her father would have extreme outbursts of anger, followed by weeks of silence when he would close himself off from the family. He tended to blame his roller-coaster emotions on her. One night, when Rue was fourteen, she came home a few minutes late for dinner after a coach had kept her team late. In a fit of anger, Rue's father screamed at Rue in front of her mother and siblings before storming out of the house. Rue felt awful, apologizing over and over, begging her father for forgiveness.

The next day, instead of apologizing for *his* behavior, Rue's dad, along with the support of Rue's mother, sat her down and explained why *her* actions were causing his angry outbursts. He asked her to memorize Scripture verses related to disobedient children. She needed to be careful never to break a rule in order to become an obedient daughter. He then prayed for her heart to change. According to him, any time *he* lashed out in anger, it was because *Rue* had dishonored God.

Over time the rules became increasingly rigid, and all her attempts to abide by them did nothing to stop her dad's anger. Rue finally had enough. She refused to apologize for her father's anger that fateful night of the texting. And her parents promptly kicked her out.

Rue clawed her way forward in life, relying on her talent, smarts, and charisma to help her to appear "normal" to other people, even though she felt decimated inside. She'd earned a scholarship to play sports in college and never told anyone why her parents didn't show up to watch her play. She had even found her way into a relationship with a man who loved her. But despite her living away from home and separating physically from her parents' toxicity, the residue of trauma still remained in her body, especially when she engaged in spiritual practices.

Spiritual wounds can cut to the core of who you are. They wound you in the most sacred, vulnerable place inside, causing you to question your inherent worth as a beloved child of God. They can also cause you to question God altogether.

As we've discussed, your parents or early caregivers provided your first glimpse of connectedness and safety when you were young. If they loved you well, you caught a glimpse of what God is like. If they abused, neglected, or harmed you, it created a spiritual wound, often damaging your perception of God.

Rue hadn't left her faith. But when the people who were supposed to love and guide her turned on her—in the name of God—parts of her couldn't distinguish between the real God and a false representation of God she was shown.

Why is this type of spiritual wound so awful? There are two primary reasons:

1. You are being shamed and hurt, which is hard enough.
2. You are being shamed and hurt by someone who claims the authority of the most powerful being in the universe.

It's compounded trauma—trauma upon trauma. All trauma causes you to question your worth. But spiritual trauma adds the terrorizing layer that God might question your worth too. That is incredibly wrong. Consider the words of Jesus: "If anyone causes one of these little ones—those who believe in me—to stumble, it would be better for them if a large millstone were hung around their neck and they were thrown into the sea."[1]

Your experience might not be as overt as Rue's. But there are countless ways that childhood wounds can affect the way you see God. For instance, if your parents talked about God's love while never making time for you, a part of you may have picked up the idea that God is distant. Or if a parent's love was based on performance, you will likely think God's love is performance based too.[2]

Another complicating factor is that faith-based interactions may reignite the pain. Specific words and spiritual practices that seem normal to everyone else might bring up painful feelings within you. For example, if someone betrayed your trust while claiming to "pray" for you, their actions could make the practice of group prayer feel uncomfortable to you. Likewise, certain Bible verses may have been used to manipulate you, which might bring up painful feelings when you hear those passages, even when they are not being misused.

It can be incredibly hard to disentangle the spiritual messages you received from the reality of what is true about God. Rationally, you might know that God is good and cares for you. But parts of you don't really trust God—and you certainly don't trust yourself.

Toxic shame enters your mind, and you might start wondering, *How could my parents or spiritual leaders be wrong? What if I'm the problem? What if I deserved what I got?* Your relationship with God—and with yourself—is completely disrupted.

Please hear me say: *it's not your fault.*

Steps to Heal from Spiritual Wounds

If you're struggling with the pain of a spiritual wound, you're not alone. If someone misrepresented God to you through toxic actions or words, you are in the center of God's love *and* God's justice—whether you feel that or not. God hates injustice with you.

You can start the healing process by taking these steps.

Step 1. Name spiritual abuse as a trauma.

Religious trauma is not often discussed, but it's incredibly important to name. When a parent or authority figure abuses his or her power in the name of God, it has terrible effects, such as:

- Feelings of anger, confusion, and bitterness toward God
- Toxic shame, self-denial, and self-hatred

- Unholy fear of God's wrath or punishment
- Anxiety or disassociation when it comes to spiritual practices

These reactions don't necessarily mean that you are far from God. In fact, it's the opposite! These reactions mean your body is working to protect you in the only way it knows how.

These feelings are responses embedded deep within your nervous system. You can't simply will them away. Such trauma responses require your compassionate attention, a loving witness, and a healing process. Once you understand that you are dealing with a conditioned trauma response, you can set out on a path toward healing.

Step 2. Acknowledge how you feel inside.

The experience of wanting to participate in faith practices but feeling anxious or guarded is important to notice. The solution isn't to muscle your way through the disparity. Nor is it to beat yourself up. Instead, get curious about what you notice in your body and soul. Hurting parts of you are giving you valuable information about ways you were harmed in the past. This inner tension is the beckoning voice of a wound in need of healing. There's a story inside you in need of a loving witness.

Extend compassion toward these parts of you that feel skeptical, fearful, and guarded. They're protecting you from the ways other people have misconstrued what God represents. Those feelings deserve your appreciation. God honors those parts of you too.

For example, when Rue started to get curious about the anxiety she felt at church, she realized a thousand paper cuts, combined with big gashes, had left gaping wounds in the way she experienced God. Parts of her longed to feel close to God. But other parts of her didn't know who the real God was. Was he angry like her father? Was he scapegoating her—quietly throwing her under the bus—like her mother? How could she possibly know what the love of a good, trustworthy God felt like, when all she'd known was judgment and blame? The disparity between what she had been taught about God versus what she had been shown in her home created deep internal tension.

These conflicting feelings didn't mean she was doing anything wrong. They were evidence she was hurting. As Rue honored these feelings with compassion, those parts of her softened a bit. She experienced a glimpse of what it's like to create safety within herself.

Step 3. Rebuild your sense of safety.

The work of healing means establishing a sense of safety. The tender parts of you that carry painful memories need to sense your understanding and compassion. They need to know you will work to protect yourself from harm going forward.

It's incredibly important to be tender with the part of you that feels confused or abandoned by God. If church or spiritual practices are activating anxiety, you may need to take some time away to heal. It's painful to step away from church attendance and other faith practices. And, yes, the judgment of others can be real. But Jesus took time away to tend to himself and connect to God and a few of his close friends when religious leaders threatened him.[3] You may need to follow his brave example.

As you develop safety within, you can start to discern where you sense safety in other people. You might return to this formative question: *When and with whom have I felt known, safe, or seen?*

When you catch a glimpse of safety in another person, you catch a glimpse of what God is like. It might be a close friend, aunt, or therapist. It might have been a coach, pastor, or grandparent. Frankly, it might not have been a person of faith. God will

> **When you catch a glimpse of safety in another person, you catch a glimpse of what God is like.**

use the most surprising ways to show you glimpses of the love he has for you.

As Rue and I discussed where she felt a sense of spiritual safety, she laughed. "Honestly? I feel safest when I'm out with my agnostic friends and we start talking about God. There's no judgment, no shame. Just real conversation about what God might be like. In those moments, I know God is real. I know God is different from the way my parents described him."

There was nothing trivial about what Rue shared. In fact, it was the sacred soil of healing. In stumbling upon a group of people who were genuinely curious and open about what she believed about God, Ruestumbled upon a glimpse of spiritual safety.

This can be true for you as well.

We are incarnational beings—we bring Christ to one another in our embodied presence. We do it imperfectly, of course, but when we experience goodness, safety, or love in another person, we start to heal.

Hang on to that feeling of safety in your body, in your memory. Dwell on it in your heart and mind. This is no accident. This experience of safety is as real as every moment of shame. As Solomon said in the book Song of Solomon, "Love is as strong as death."[4]

Step 4. Separate the God you were shown from God's character.

Over time you can begin to disentangle the God who loves you from the misrepresentation of God by toxic people. As you are ready, you might consider who God is apart from the hurtful actions of others. For instance:

- God loves justice, mercy, and humility (Micah 6:8).
- God comforts the grief-stricken and the brokenhearted (Matthew 5:4).

"easier to find God inside ourselves instead of looking for him in created things."[8] Your spiritual practices must take into account the wounded part of you. Moving toward glimpses of love and of safety will lead you home—home to yourself and home to God.

This is what Rue discovered. As she gave herself permission to grieve the false representations of God she'd been shown, she grew stronger inside. She began to notice ways she was drawn to other people who found themselves bitter and disenchanted. A tremendous ability to advocate for others who were hurting was born inside of her. She began to minister to those outside of church walls, simply by showing up authentically. To this day, both she and her husband have given hope to countless spiritual orphans, each in their own way.

God is so much more than the crummy representations handed down to you by wounded others. As you heal the wounds—and allow distance from the wounders—you might discover a God who surprises you.

Don't rush this process.

God meets you in those places where you feel real, alive, and tender. God does not force, control, or manipulate you. God wants to restore the goodness in your life that was taken away by an abusive person, group, or faith community. Whether you sense it or not, here's what is true: the God of the universe is fighting for you.

God is on your side.

Untangling Spiritual Codependency

You may not have experienced spiritual trauma like Rue did. You may have been raised in a home or faith community where God's love was taught and shown in numerous ways.

But you still may have learned to relate to God in unhealthy ways. In fact, I believe many people have developed codependent tendencies in the way they hide behind God instead of becoming true to the person God made. And I believe this is a tendency God is constantly working to heal.

Here are some questions that may point to spiritual codependency.

- Do you work hard to make sure you don't lose God's love?
- Do you struggle with decision-making because you can't figure out what God wants you to do?
- Do you dismiss a talent or longing because you think denying parts of yourself makes God happy?

None of these tendencies reflects the loving partnership God designed for us. Yet I see these tendencies in many of the women I counsel, and I have also worked to heal from these tendencies in myself. Here are some of the phrases I've noticed that, though well-intended, are worth deeper examination.

- "All I need is God."
- "I exist to serve others."
- "I must become small so that God will shine."[9]

As a young woman of faith, I tried to apply these messages quite literally through burying talents, focusing on other people in relationships, and turning to God as my "one and only" source of help. In fact, when I look back at this younger version of me, it can feel painful at times. It's sort of like watching a movie where the heroine is on the verge of self-sabotage.

I loved God, and I sensed God's love for me. But some part of me picked up the idea that "I" shouldn't matter. If "I" wanted something, that was "self"—and "self" was bad. I assumed that following God meant that I must completely obliterate any sense of "I" altogether.[10]

Misconstrued church messages combined with my childhood wounds to create unhealthy patterns of behavior that eventually led to a breakdown. Thankfully, God continued to work to bring forth the real me—through several healing relationships and a wonderful faith community.

The truth is, I meet a lot of women who operate in this way. Instead of facing fears and taking risks, we hide God-given aspects of who we are in the name of faith. Notice how easy it is to fall into this trap:

- "All I need is God" can mask "I don't know how to let others in."
- "I exist only to serve others" can mask "I don't know who I am."
- "I'll make myself small so God will shine" can mask "I'm afraid I might fail, so I'll hold myself back."

Instead of maturing into women with a strong sense of self, we are encouraged to stay hidden. I do not believe this is the kind of relationship God wants to have with us.

Instead, God wants to empower you to become your true self, the most beautiful version of the person he made. This means learning to honor the part *you* have to play in bringing forth your purpose, talents, and potential in this life you've been given.

From Hidden to Brave

Many of us want to stay like children with God—and I don't mean that we want to keep that childlike sense of wonder that Jesus means for us to have. Instead, we want to stay emotionally young because we never got that wise, on-the-ground parenting, that initial safe haven we longed for. We want assurance. We want permission. We want the path laid out in front of us. These longings make sense. And God meets us at the exact point of care that we need. But as we heal our sense of self and grow stronger inside, our relationship with God grows too.[11] In fact, sometimes, like a good parent, God nudges us gently out of the nest.

Imagine yourself as a parent caring for a baby. When the baby is young, she is fully dependent on you. Without your care, this baby would not survive. As she grows and develops into a young child, slowly she can do more for herself. She feeds herself and picks out her own clothes. At some point, she leaves the safety of your presence and heads off to school. This child is still dependent on you, but the nature of that dependence has changed. You no longer feed or dress her. Instead, you have taught her how to be brave.

Eventually, this child gets older. She's a teenager with new ideas of her own. You don't love all her ideas, but you also want to know her. You care what she has to say. You listen to her thoughtfully, even as you maintain certain guardrails to keep her safe.

Finally, this child is fully grown. She has entered adulthood. She still comes to you with challenges and to catch up on all the news. You want to honor the confidence she's gained. You try not to tell her what to do. Instead, you listen and offer insight based on the wisdom you have gleaned. You help her flesh out what she's thinking. You might share with her concerns that you have about options she's considering. You also acknowledge that there is not only one road to take.

You've equipped her. You've loved her. You've cared for her. Now here she is. She's not perfect; she makes mistakes. But overall, she is magnificent. She's demonstrating the fruit of a wise and thoughtful inner life. She knows how to look out for herself. She's not foolish; she's wise. She's building a solid foundation of relationships.

She's left your nest and is building her own life. Yet you remain connected. You delight in her presence. You still long to hear her voice. You drop everything when she shows up at your house or calls you on the phone. And you also honor the independent young woman she has become. Over many years, you have shifted from being her decision maker to her sounding board. Your relationship remains strong.

Why would our relationship with God be any different?

Why would God continue to spoon-feed us instead of equipping us to grow our own wings?[12]

Why would God push us back into the nest instead of helping us learn to fly?

I believe that God wants us to mature into thoughtful, wise adults with strong character.[13] That means he doesn't tell us what to do all the time or give us easy solutions to the problems we face.[14] Instead, God honors the work that has been cultivated deep within over time. God stays *with* us, before us, behind us, beside us,[15] even as he takes pride in seeing us develop into strong, light-bearing women.

Is it possible that God might be nudging you out of the nest, even as he stays close by? Is it possible that he wants you to learn to trust yourself, even as you stay connected to him?

How to Heal Codependent Tendencies with God

Healthy dependence on God doesn't mean you ignore the work that is yours to do in creating the life you desire. It means you invite God into every step of the process, even as you accept your responsibility to grow.

As you engage in this process, here are some steps to consider.

1. Own your role in crafting your life.

When it comes to creating your life, it's partly your work and partly God's work—plus a good dose of help from people around you.

The chart on the next page illustrates an example of what these different roles look like.

YOUR ROLE	GOD'S PROMISE
Become aware of your feelings, your body, and the conditioning you have received.	Work in you by the power of God's Spirit to help you see yourself clearly.
Identify the voice of shame.	Hold up the mirror of truth that is never shaming.
Ask for what you need from experts or people you trust.	Help you discern the advice you receive.
Take steps toward changing things you can.	Work out justice in the areas where you don't have control.
Get back up when you stumble or falter.	Meet you with grace.
Create rhythms that are good for your heart, mind, and body.	Help you heal and discover joy, peace, patience, goodness, and love.

Step 2. Employ the power of *and*.

God works miraculously *and* God works through practicality. If you notice yourself begging God for a miracle or a direct answer to a problem, consider how the following prayers use the word *and*:

- "God, grant me health *and* I'll care for my body the best way I know."
- "God, please help my friend who is suffering *and* I'll show up with a meal."
- "God, please heal this depression *and* I'm going to see a counselor."
- "God, please guide me *and* I'll research various options before making this decision."
- "God, I need your help *and* I'll ask a friend for help too."

Partnering with God means learning to ask for what we need from other people. We need wise teachers, doctors, and scientists. We need our friends. Other people need us too.

That's the beauty of breaking free from hiding behind a God we've made small. As we grow big inside and become our true selves, God is big enough to meet us there.

What if God's been there all along?

- God is with you when you enter that room full of strangers.
- God is with you as you determine if you can trust that new friend.
- God is with you as you walk into a therapist's office.

But you, dear reader, have to take that first step.

Step 3. Take the first step.

After graduating from college, I struggled with a vocational decision. I had analyzed the decision from every angle for months. One afternoon, I told the therapist who was supervising my counseling internship, "I just wish God would tell me what to do." This mentor said something I've never forgotten: Sometimes, God directs a person in motion.

Sometimes, God directs a person in motion.

Through this mentor, God was gently saying to me, *Take a step toward what you think is best. I will join you there.* It was his way of bringing life to the words of Proverbs: "In their hearts, humans plan their course, but the LORD establishes their steps."[16] Proverbs 16:9

That day, I decided to take a step to apply to a counseling program, and that very first step led to the work I am doing to this day. It led to you reading this book.

On another occasion, I was turning myself inside out to ascertain God's will for a difficult dating relationship. For months, I vacillated back and forth: *Should I stay or should I walk away?* God would not tell me what to do. During this conundrum, my mom said to me, "God doesn't play guessing games with us." She astutely figured out that I was blaming my indecision on God. The truth was, I'd been talking to God, but I'd been afraid to voice my concerns to the man I was dating. When I finally did, his response gave me valuable information. (We broke up.)

In this case, my mom brought to life another wise proverb: "Commit to the LORD whatever you do, and he will establish your plans."[17] Prov. 16:3

In both of these cases, I had to use my head, listen to my heart, and pray for guidance—even as I took steps to express my voice. I gained wisdom as a result of walking with God *into* these confusing situations instead of waiting for answers to drop from the sky. I learned more about myself, and I learned more about God.

The way through a tricky situation shows up as you take one brave step at a time.

Maturity means using our minds, the wisdom we have gained, and the best resources available to make hard decisions. That doesn't mean we stop depending on God. Instead, as our relationship grows, we depend on God in new ways. In fact, we begin to see God as the best sort of partner—one who is always with us.

Together with God

As you've read this book, you've learned how to trust yourself, how to find your voice, and how to become your true self. This doesn't mean letting go of God. In fact, you couldn't discover your true self apart from God.

God is still your Rescuer, your Rock, your Provider. Don't mistake what I'm saying. But don't underestimate *your* capability in any given situation. Let me give you a real-time example of what healthy dependence has started to look like in my life.

Right now, as I type these words, I sense God's presence with me. My eyes are not closed. I'm not talking directly to him. I'm typing and thinking and engaging my mind. I'm doing my part, which is drawing on years of research and work with clients, of prayer and self-reflection. I am here. And God is here. We're not merged, but we're not separate. We are working in synergy. We're in this work together.

That's not to say I'm writing these words perfectly or that I'm in some kind of mystical, otherworldly place. I'm not. My feet are cold, and I'm frustrated with the slow speed of my computer! But with an almost imperceptible blink of awareness—an inhale or a glance at the beauty of the tree outside my window—*God is here. More of my true self is here.* The more I've grown into myself, the more I sense God. The more I sense God, the more I connect to the best of me inside. It's an unending dance of connectedness and autonomy.

This is the dance of dependence I wish for you—*for all of eternity.*

Becoming your true self goes hand in hand with trusting the One who made you.

It's taking responsibility for your own life in partnership with God and in partnership with the people you've chosen to place around you.

Instead of hiding behind God's bigness, you *lean into* God's bigness everywhere you go. You lean into the bigness inside you. You honor yourself and honor your maker.

This is what it means to heal.

This is what it means to surrender.

This is opening yourself to hope and to wonder.

This is being alive.

This is worship.

This is becoming the best of you, with God's help.

Reflections

1. What did you notice inside as you read the section on spiritual abuse? Are there any spiritual practices you've been avoiding as a result of a spiritual wound?
2. Consider the following questions:
   - Where do you feel most alive?
   - Where do you sense love?
   - Where, and with whom, do you feel safety?
3. Have you felt a sense of hiding behind God? In what way might God be nudging you to take a brave step?

PART 4

Live the Best of You

It is quite true what philosophy says, that life must be understood backwards. But then one forgets the other principle: that it must be lived forwards.

—Søren Kierkegaard, *Papers and Journals*

Chapter 11

How Will I Know I've Arrived?

Envisioning the Best of You

HOW DO I KNOW I'M READY?" MY CLIENT JESSICA ASKED.

Jessica had come to see me to work through the grief of losing her mom when she was a baby. Her dad and stepmom had done the best that they could, but as a young woman, she'd been noticing sadness deep inside. She rarely spoke of her mom. Instead, she was adept at putting on rose-colored glasses, stubbornly looking for the positive side of everything. But, as the untended grief inside mounted, she reached out to me.

After a year of meeting together, she had faced her grief bravely. She still had a sunny aspect to her disposition, but she could also honor her pain. In addition, she had made several proactive changes in her life. Jessica forged a relationship with her aunt—her mom's sister—who she now kept in touch with regularly. With her friends, she learned that she could be both a fun-loving buddy *and* open up about her pain. She had also become intentional about dating, identifying a clear picture of the qualities she needed in a partner. Finally, she had made a major career decision that aligned with her giftings and inner longings.

Jessica had created space for grief and was equipped to create the life she desired.

But it wasn't all this work that made Jessica "ready" for the future. Instead, Jessica was ready because she had replaced rose-colored glasses with what I call *hopeful curiosity.*

Hopeful curiosity is a way of looking at the world that honors the agency you have *and* the reality that life can surprise you in both good and bad ways. It's believing in the best of you while staying curious about the challenges that will still come your way.

The truth is, I worry most about the people who tell me, "I'm all set. I've got it in the bag."

Here's a tip from a therapist: people who are convinced they've "arrived" aren't there yet.

How do you know when you've "arrived" at the best of who you are? The answer is a paradox: you know that you've arrived when you're aware that you haven't. In fact, you know that you've arrived when you can hold two ideas side by side in yourself:

1. *I am equipped. I have what it takes.*
2. *I will face setbacks. I will make mistakes.*

You know you're becoming the best of you when you

- acknowledge painful emotions *and* have confidence in your ability to face them.
- consistently express your own voice *and* consider input from trusted people.
- make peace with your strengths *and* the struggles you still face.
- stop looking to others for rescue *and* identify wise people to keep by your side.
- honor your needs *and* give from strength to other people.

You know you've arrived when you discover that you're stepping out of your conditioning—out from under your invisibility cloak—and showing up as the real you with other people in your life. You increasingly show regard for yourself. You take brave steps each day toward authentic actions and responses. Soon, your body and soul start to remember these new ways. For example, you

- *remember* what it was like to let that painful emotion wash over you *before* you reacted.
- *remember* how proud you felt of yourself after you initiated a hard conversation.
- *remember* what it was like to trust yourself enough to heed a red flag.
- *remember* the voice of that tender one inside who needed your compassion.
- *remember* how it felt when you said yes to your own healing.

Remembering says, "I *did* that. That is who I am."

I wrote this chapter for you as a blessing and as a charge—to remind you that you are prepared to say yes to this beautiful life God has given you.

Surf the Waves of Emotions

Trouble will come your way. But you know how to face what is hard. You have what it takes.

You now understand that the best of you does not pretend you are all set. Nor do you walk around in a pleasant state of blissful neutrality. That's certainly not the example we see in Jesus, a man who experienced anger, anguish, and heartbreak as well as delight.

You'll still experience a range of emotions like fear, sadness, anger, and joy. But the best of you knows that these emotions make you human—a living, breathing glimpse of heaven. The best of you trusts that you can navigate the challenges that will come your way with skill and integrity.

Other people might try to discount this new way of honoring yourself. For example, friends or family members might try to get you to go back to the old way of burying pain instead of bravely facing it. But you know better now. You no longer betray yourself or bypass your pain. Instead, you bear spiritual fruit—love, joy, peace, patience, kindness, goodness, self-control, gentleness, and faithfulness[1]—toward other people *and* toward yourself.

You understand the difference between spiritual fruit and spiritual bypassing:

SPIRITUAL FRUIT	SPIRITUAL BYPASSING
I still feel anxious, but I can now be *gentle* and *patient* with myself.	Starve your fear. It's the enemy of your faith!
When I'm hurt, I am learning to be *kind* to myself.	You shouldn't feel hurt—pray it away.
I have doubts, and I *faithfully* talk about them with God.	You wouldn't have doubts if your faith was stronger.
I love and care for others, as I *love* and care for the tender one inside of me.	It's better to be selfless—you should only focus on other people.
My anger is valid, and I use it for *good* in my own life and for other people. I know how to harness its power.	Anger is bad.
I experience *joy*, because I'm at *peace* with myself.	Choose joy! (Said with fists clenched.)

You no longer need to give in to painful emotions, nor do you deny them. Instead, you surf those emotions like a wave passing by. You slow down, steady yourself, breathe deeply, and wait, knowing that the wave will run its course. You get curious about these inner feelings. You acknowledge them honestly as you show kindness and compassion toward yourself.

Express Your Voice

The best of you reveals the beauty inside of you through the power of your voice. You no longer need that cloak of pleasing, performing, producing, and pretending. You no longer need to peace-keep and permission-seek incessantly. Instead, you know how to express your voice in a healthy way. You realize deep down that what you have to say matters. You identify the voice of ego instead of acting out of it. You recognize shame's wily ways and do not succumb to them. Finally, you honor the tender places deep inside and work bravely to protect them.

Expressing your voice is the confident, consistent practice of speaking up on behalf of what you need and value in your relationships. This voice you have discovered might be soft or it might be forceful.[2] Sometimes it speaks loudest through your actions.

You also understand that expressing your own voice is not about shutting other people down. Instead, as you show up in your relationships with confidence, you become more open. You trust yourself, which means you're no longer at the mercy of others. You consider someone else's perspective without losing yours.

Expressing your voice is both vulnerable *and* powerful.

Yes, expressing your voice might offend someone else. But it also leads to deeper, more authentic connections. It will help you move *away* from the people who aren't interested in hearing from you at all and *toward* the people who value what you have to say. If the relationship is worth keeping, your voice will make it even stronger.

Please, dear reader, spend time each day listening to the stirring of your own wise voice deep inside.

Make Peace with Yourself

Another interesting paradox occurs as the best of you emerges from inside. You no longer bend yourself into contortions to appear as if you have it all together. Instead, you make peace with yourself. You make peace with yourself as you stay honest with yourself and with God.

Making peace with yourself isn't resignation nor is it naive acceptance. Instead, you understand the difference between where you are and where you hope to be. You hold that tension inside you with curiosity and compassion. You now *pause* before you please, produce, perform, perfect, or peace-keep. You ask yourself

- *Is this what I want?*
- *Does this align with who God made me to be?*

What does this process look like? Let's reflect on some of the stories from earlier in this book.

Jackie, who struggled with self-rejection, made peace with the fiery part of her that could fill her up with anger. She can now pause when she notices a fight response, before she lashes out. She is an exceptional advocate for herself, her children, and other people. Shame has lost its hold in her life.

Gina, who had gotten lost in a maze of anxiety, made peace with the cues her body gives her when she overextends her schedule. She has learned to pay attention to these cues and honor them by cultivating life-giving activities.

Jessica, who had buried pain from the loss of her mom, made peace with her grief, even as she embraced her sunny disposition. She recognized that she could be a fun-loving person *and* someone who could honor her own pain.

And I've made peace with the voice of my conditioning to always please other people. Each day I grow stronger in pausing to check inside myself *before* I commit or communicate. I can also apologize and course correct when I make mistakes.

You make peace with yourself as you stop justifying old patterns of behavior.

You make peace with yourself as you turn toward healing and the possibility of growth and change.

You make peace with yourself as you honor the presence of both your beauty *and* your blind spots.

Make Friends with Yourself

As you make peace with yourself, you start to notice the presence of a wonderful new friend. Suddenly, *you've* become somebody who is enjoyable to spend time with.

It's amazing to feel connected to a friend, parent, child, or spouse. But it's equally amazing to add yourself to the list of people with whom you experience a warm connection. As you make friends with yourself, you discover a sense of safety within. You still need other people, but you also know how to be kind to yourself when you are hurting or down.

> **Making friends with yourself means learning what brings you life.**

Making friends with yourself means learning what brings you life.

Remember the story of Leah? After her relationship with Chuck ended, she landed in a fixer-upper house, living by herself for the first time. The silence felt deafening at first. She was brokenhearted and reeling from the years of toxicity she'd ingested. Instead of drowning out the pain with a quick-fix relationship, she and I worked together to help her make friends with herself.

Leah started by going out to see movies on her own. It seemed simple enough, but it was an important exercise for her. She had always watched movies as if she was experiencing it through the eyes and ears of the person next to her. When she went by herself, she got to figure out what she was experiencing in response to the story on the screen.

She also began to fix up her house and realized how much she enjoyed it. After work, she'd come home and paint a section of a wall. When that was finished, she tackled the project of ripping up old carpet, then changing out the bathroom tile. She watched YouTube videos and learned from social media DIYers. It took nearly a year, but over time that house became a source of peace and joy for her. She put her own set of fingerprints on it, and she learned what safety feels like.

Finally, she began to learn what kind of people she enjoyed. For example, one night she went out to dinner with some single friends her age. They were nice enough, but she told me she felt restless and disinterested in what they were talking about. She was just as happy to get home to enjoy the haven she had built for herself.

Leah was shocked when I suggested that she wasn't obligated to prefer someone's company just because they wanted hers. Intrigued by this new revelation, Leah began to notice whose company she did enjoy. It turned out the person she enjoyed most was her eighty-year-old neighbor—a vivacious, redheaded woman who told stories that made Leah laugh out loud. This woman was a survivor, and listening to her stories made Leah feel hopeful and alive.

Instead of trying to fit in with what was expected of her, she began to ask herself

- *Whose company do I enjoy?*
- *Who or what brings out the best of me?*

Leah learned a key lesson: if you want authentic connection with others, make friends with yourself.

Live at Peace with Other People

As you've grown stronger, you now know that living at peace with others includes being faithful to yourself. You can't find peace in your relationships until you show up as your true self.

Living at peace with others includes paying attention to what you need to stay healthy in your relationships. It may mean bravely negotiating change with someone you love. Or it might mean staying distant from someone who is not able to tolerate or respect your boundaries.

Here's the kicker: sometimes, living at peace with other people means living at peace with disappointing them.

Most of us hate disappointing other people. It goes right back to that cocktail of codependency—we are conditioned to hitch our self-worth to how well we make other people feel. But what if you measured your worth by living from integrity? It's incredibly important to balance your responsibility to others with a deep sense of responsibility to yourself. It's not only good for you; it's good for other people.

As demonstrated in the Gospels, Jesus disappointed people frequently.[3] Jesus didn't always act in the way his followers wanted, yet he was the Prince of Peace. Jesus didn't disappoint people because he was selfish. He disappointed people because he lived with integrity. He always acted out of a commitment to a higher good. He modeled how to

- focus on what God wanted, not on pleasing others;
- stay true to his calling, not on temporary distractions; and
- see the big picture instead of settling for instant gratification.

There is a lesson here for us.

As you embrace the best of you, in partnership with God, you might disappoint someone. But that doesn't necessarily mean you are doing something wrong. You can act with integrity. You have built trust with yourself, and that trust now speaks volumes to other people. For example, you now know how to do some amazing things.

- You can anchor yourself in the yes you are saying to yourself and to God.
- You can express your conviction. For example, you might say:
  - "As hard as it is, I've arrived at this conclusion."
  - "In order to honor my existing commitments, I have to say no to this one."
  - "I need to focus on [my work, my family, my health]."
- You can honor their perspective without apologizing unnecessarily, getting defensive, or backtracking. You might simply say, "I understand," "I get it," "I know this is hard."
- You can remove yourself from toxicity. It's never okay for the disappointed person to become abusive. If their response turns toxic, you're prepared with new skills.

As you honor both yourself and other people, you start to show up in the same way Jesus has shown up for you—with honesty, love, and intentionality. You are anchored in your own integrity, which equips you to show up far more effectively with others, even when you disappoint them.

You're not supposed to meet every need around you. Every need is not your call to serve.

You're not supposed to meet every need around you. Every need is not your call to serve. And the truth is, another person won't meet all your needs either.

As you attempt to make peace with others, here's a prayer that I find helpful:[4]

God, give me the courage to stop pleasing others,
    the confidence to show up as my true self,
      and the wisdom to know how to live at peace with others
without betraying myself.

Envision the Best of You

Before we close, take a moment to envision your future. Think about the woman God designed you to be. Imagine yourself free of the weight of your pain, a future version of yourself who has moved through the darkness and found an even better place. Envision her in detail.

What does she look like?

What is she doing?

Where is she?

Who is with her?

The best of you is waiting for you.

The best of you doesn't hide or pretend. Instead, she shows up as she really is. She's creative and courageous. She has confidence. She cares for others with intention.

The best of you is humble but never self-rejecting.

The best of you bravely uses her voice, even when it's vulnerable.

The best of you is curious, not critical.

The best of you understands that what she's going through is only one part of her story, not the sum total of who she is.

The best of you knows she is a beautiful reflection of God's very image.

The best of you listens for the tender one inside.

The best of you knows

- you are held.
- you are seen.

- you are enough.
- no one can take your place on this earth.

The best of you knows you are more capable than you think and God is closer than you feel.

The best of you is not perfection. It's not the absence of anger, grief, or fear. The best of you is presence. It's honoring your unique experience.

As you envision the best of you, here's the irony: she's already inside you, waiting for you to release her into the world. The best of you has been inside you all along. You may have lost sight of her, but she's been with you. Maybe you lost sight of her as you worked overtime helping others. Maybe you lost sight of her as you coped with pain through numbing. Maybe you lost sight of her at church or at home or as the voice of shame took over. Maybe you lost sight of her as you tried to find yourself in other people's love.

But she's been in there all along.

God put her inside of you. She's yours to unleash. Uncovering the best of you is your most important work.

She'll lead you out from hiding.

She'll transform your pain and your loneliness.

She'll gently mitigate your efforts to win love.

She knows who you were before it all got so messed up.

She knows who you were before the world beat you up.

Envisioning the best of you is the starting point for becoming the woman God made you to become. It's how you learn to ward off danger and pull in the good things you need. It's how you find your way to solid ground.

Envisioning the best of you is how you find your way through pain. It's how you heal your broken heart and become more rooted where you stand.

Envisioning the best of you is how you rediscover joy. It's how you unbury lost desires and hold them wide open to the sky. It's how you love others without losing yourself. It's how you embody Jesus by living out of your true self.

This is the message I have for you as you move into this wide-open life ahead of you:

Envision the best of you.

Envision the best of you, because that is where you will find God.

Reflections

1. Imagine the best of you in the future. It could be one, five, or ten years from now. Choose whatever increment of time feels helpful to you.[5]
2. How would the future version of you understand the current situation you are facing?
3. How would *she* respond in this situation?
4. What qualities does that version of you have readily available to her? (It might be wisdom, confidence, strength, courage, calm, kindness, or playfulness.)

Conclusion

AS I PUT THE FINISHING TOUCHES ON THE FIRST DRAFT OF this manuscript, it is approaching the year anniversary of that night I could not connect to my finger and then to the whole left side of my body—the night I had a stroke.

In the weeks leading up to the anniversary of that night, countless tiny details evoked anxiety—activities like taking a walk, putting makeup on my left finger, or planning a Friday night date with my husband. Colors and smells also brought forth anxiety, such as the way the sun burns orange in late August, the shorter days, the smoky haze from nearby wildfires, the scent of hay in the air.

And my mind started to connect dots that don't really go together.

None of these things—not putting on makeup, not the scent of wildfires, not the shortening of days—actually caused my stroke. But this is the way of trauma. The body remembers. It takes in all the sights and smells surrounding a frightening, painful event, and it creates a story.

Our body does what it is designed to do. It warns us of danger by alerting us to signals that it has paired with danger—even when those signals aren't actually dangerous anymore.

What's powerful is that you are also designed to heal. As you engage your conscious mind, the real you inside, you can lovingly attend to the cues your body gives you. As a result, you can undo its subconscious ways of connecting dots and create a new story, a truer story based on the person you have yet to become.

Life is all too often busted wide open. It's messy.

And yet our ability to heal, by design, is beautiful.

Things happen that scare us, that hurt us, that make us realize we are vulnerable, that make us realize we don't ultimately have control. Things happen that are hard, that can change our lives forever.

Memories of those painful events lodge inside us. And our bodies do what they are supposed to do. They remember. They remind us that we are vulnerable.

I had always wanted to be rescued from this kind of vulnerability—from a stroke, from loneliness, from toxic relationships, from any painful aspect of life. But God simply would not rescue me. Instead, God has patiently, lovingly guided me into a journey of becoming more brave, more authentic, and more open to both the beauty and the brokenness that exist side by side.

I have learned to value that vulnerability, not shove it aside. I now know how to turn *toward* myself, to pay attention to the cues my body and soul are sending me. I know how to become aware of the tender one inside me so I can gently lead her.

I can honor the embodied soul that God has given me. I can give her love and compassion. I can ask God to be with her. And I can ask other people to bear witness to her pain, so she never has to walk alone.

I can write a new story weaving together threads of a burnt orange sun and the smoky haze of wildfires into a tapestry of courage, of strength, and of a commitment to inhabiting the heck out of this life I still have yet to live.

I can open my palms wide up to the sky and say:

God, it is you. It is you who numbers my days. I surrender to all that you are. And I will also relentlessly live this life you have given me while I am still here. I will no longer hide out of fear. I will no longer play small to stay safe.

Instead, I will show up for this life each and every day.

I will show up to write words, to create.

I will show up to care for my body, to nourish my soul each day.

I will show up to love others with purpose and with thanks.

I will continue to live boldly while I still have days.

I will continue to live in the tension of what is hard and what is achingly beautiful.

I will continue to heal.

Acknowledgments

TO MY TEACHERS AND MENTORS: CRAIG, GARY AND MARK, Stacy and Tim, Jeffrey, Diana, Ellen, and Kate—you have given me a thousand glimpses of what God is like. Thank you. To Rachel Jacobson, Rob Eagar, Elizabeth Cunningham, and Jenny Baumgartner for your invaluable contributions at various points in the manuscript development and to the amazing Thomas Nelson publishing family: thank you for believing in me. To Kate Wilder: thank you for your steady and wise presence throughout the process of writing.

To my colleagues Rebecca and Aundi, Chuck, Jenna, Tammy, Peter, and Kim: I am grateful for you. The light that you shine into this work that we do as therapists and writers brings constant glimmers of hope. To my clients: bearing witness to your stories has been my deepest honor. To my friends from Wyoming to Dartmouth and Denver, from LA to Boston and beyond: I love you. You have shown faithfulness through so many different seasons of my life. Thank you for loving me.

To my mom, dad, Courtney, John, and Veronica: because of you, I know what goodness feels like. And to my family: Brooke and Chase, thank you for showing me what it means to be both kind and true. To my husband, Joe: you bring out the best of me.

To God: thank you for the most surprising gift of my life—the freedom that flows from a spacious soul that is *known*.

Notes

Chapter 1: What Do You Want?

1. Jesus didn't bypass the self when he said, *"Love your neighbor as yourself"* (Matthew 22:39). His teaching suggests that learning to regard yourself is key to learning to love others.
2. For more on setting boundaries, see the groundbreaking book by Henry Cloud and John Townsend, *Boundaries: When to Say Yes, How to Say No to Take Control of Your Life* (Grand Rapids: Zondervan, 1992).
3. Genesis 1:27.
4. Ephesians 2:10.
5. Carl Jung, "Christ, a Symbol of the Self," in *The Collected Works of C. G. Jung*, vol. 9, part 2, trans. Gerhard Adler and R. F. C. Hull (Princeton, NJ: Princeton University Press, 1959), 37.
6. Matthew 5:37.
7. Matthew 16:24–26.
8. Matthew 20:32; John 1:38.

Chapter 2: How Did I Get Here?

1. Codependency was first conceptualized by Dr. Karen Horney, in what she called a "moving toward" personality type. See Karen Horney, *Our Inner Conflicts: A Constructive Theory of Neurosis* (New York: Routledge, 2013). It was popularized by Melody Beattie in her 1986 book *Codependent No More: How to Stop Controlling Others and Start Caring for Yourself* (Center City, MN: Hazelden, 1986).

2. Saint Augustine famously prayed, "Let me know Thee even as I am known." Saint Augustine, *The Confessions of St. Augustine*, trans. Rex Warner (New York: Penguin Books, 1963), 210. And John Calvin wrote, "Our wisdom . . . consists almost entirely of two parts: the knowledge of God and of ourselves. But as these are connected together by many ties, it is not easy to determine which of the two precedes and gives birth to the other." John Calvin, *Institutes of the Christian Religion* (Grand Rapids: Eerdmans, 1957), 1:37.

3. For more on trauma, see Bessel van der Kolk's *The Body Keeps the Score: Brain, Mind, and Body in the Healing of Trauma* (New York: Viking, 2014) and Peter A. Levine's *In an Unspoken Voice: How the Body Releases Trauma and Restores Goodness* (Berkeley, CA: North Atlantic Books, 2010).

4. This book focuses on the psychological and spiritual impact of trauma. For more on the medical effects of trauma, see Nadine Burke Harris, *The Deepest Well: Healing the Long-Term Effects of Childhood Adversity* (Boston: Mariner, 2018).

5. For an overview of various forms of racial trauma, see Sheila Wise Rowe, *Healing Racial Trauma: The Road to Resilience* (Downers Grove, IL: InterVarsity Press, 2020).

6. Bessel van der Kolk, *The Body Keeps the Score: Brain, Mind, and Body in the Healing of Trauma* (New York: Viking, 2014), 143.

7. Maurizio Benazzo and Zaya Benazzo, *The Wisdom of Trauma Featuring Dr. Gabor Maté*, produced by Maurizio and Zaya Benazzo from Science and Nonduality (SAND), 2021, 16:20.

8. According to the CDC, 61 percent of US adults have suffered at least one significant trauma, known as an adverse childhood experience. "Fast Facts: Preventing Adverse Childhood Experiences," Centers for Disease Control and Prevention, accessed February 21, 2022, https://www.cdc.gov/violenceprevention/aces/fastfact.html.

9. Bruce D. Perry and Oprah Winfrey discuss this question in their book *What Happened to You? Conversations on Trauma, Resilience, and Healing* (New York: Flatiron Books, 2021).

10. Aundi Kolber provides a helpful overview of trauma's impact on the nervous system in her book, *Try Softer: A Fresh Approach to Move Us Out of Anxiety, Stress, and Survival Mode—and into a Life of Connection and Joy* (Carol Stream, IL: Tyndale, 2020).

11. For more on the neurobiological effects of survival responses, see Dan Siegel, *Mindsight: The New Science of Personal Transformation* (New York: Bantam, 2010).

12. The term *fawning* is credited to therapist Pete Walker. See *Complex PTSD: From Surviving to Thriving* (Lafayette, CA: Azure Coyote, 2013).

13. Job 42:7–8; Isaiah 53:4; John 11:33; Matthew 5:3–5.

14. Diane Langberg observed that women "are taught to yield, support, and nurture," while males "are taught to be strong, competent, and in charge," resulting in *both* missing out on becoming the people God created them to be. Diane Langberg, *Redeeming Power: Understanding Authority and Abuse in the Church* (Grand Rapids: Brazos, 2020), 93.

15. According to a 2021 WHO report, nearly 1 in 3 women globally (30 percent) have experienced physical or sexual violence. See "Violence Against Women," World Health Organization, March 9, 2021, https://www.who.int/news-room/fact-sheets/detail/violence-against-women.

16. For more on women and mental health, see "Depression in Women: Understanding the Gender Gap," Mayo Clinic, accessed April 15, 2022, https://www.mayoclinic.org/diseases-conditions/depression/in-depth/depression/art-20047725; and "Women and Mental Health," updated May 2019, National Institute of Health, https://www.nimh.nih.gov/health/topics/women-and-mental-health.

17. John 15:13.

18. Psalm 139:13–16; Proverbs 4:23; John 10:10.

19. Matthew 16:24.

20. John 12:24–25 The Message.

21. John 1:11–12 The Message, emphasis added.

Chapter 3: How Do I Find My Way Out?

1. Ephesians 6:10.

2. *Oxford English Dictionary*, s.v. "trust," Lexico, accessed June 9, 2022, https://www.lexico.com/definition/trust.

3. Jeremiah 17:9 NLT.

4. Alison Cook and Kimberly Miller, *Boundaries for Your Soul: How to Turn Your Overwhelming Thoughts and Feelings into Your Greatest Allies* (Nashville: Thomas Nelson, 2018), 21–22.

5. Jeremiah 31:33, emphasis added.

6. John 14:16–17.
7. Johanna H. M. Hovenkamp-Hermelink et al., "Differential Associations of Locus of Control with Anxiety, Depression and Life-Events: A Five-Wave, Nine-Year Study to Test Stability and Change," *Journal of Affective Disorders* 253 (June 2019): 26–34.
8. Bessel van der Kolk, *The Body Keeps the Score* (New York: Viking, 2014), 113.
9. Sefa Awaworyi Churchill et al., "Locus of Control and the Gender Gap in Mental Health," *Journal of Economic Behavior and Organization* 178 (2020): 740–58.
10. Yasmin Iles-Caven et al., "The Relationship Between Locus of Control and Religious Behavior and Beliefs in a Large Population of Parents: An Observational Study," *Frontiers in Psychology* 11 (2020): 1462.
11. Matthew 25:14–30; Ephesians 4:14–16; 1 Corinthians 14:20.
12. Curt Thompson, *The Soul of Shame: Retelling the Stories We Believe About Ourselves* (Downers Grove, IL: InterVarsity Press, 2015), 55.

Chapter 4: What Am I Really Like?

1. *Trailhead* is a term used in IFS therapy, created by Richard C. Schwartz, *Introduction to the Internal Family Systems Model* (Oak Park, IL: Trailheads, 2001).
2. For a helpful application of the Enneagram, see Beth McCord and Jeff McCord, *More Than Your Number: A Christ-Centered Enneagram Approach to Becoming AWARE of Your Internal World* (Nashville: Thomas Nelson, 2022).
3. Erik Erikson, *Childhood and Society* (New York: W. W. Norton, 1993).
4. Attachment theory is based on the work of J. Bowlby, *Attachment and Loss*, vol. 1, *Attachment* (New York: Basic Books, 1969); and M. D. Ainsworth et al., *Patterns of Attachment: A Psychological Study of the Strange Situation* (Hillsdale, NJ: Lawrence Erlbaum Associates, 1978).
5. Brené Brown discusses belonging in depth in *Braving the Wilderness: The Quest for True Belonging and the Courage to Stand Alone* (New York: Random House, 2017).
6. For more on healing the effects of racism, see Latasha Morrison, *Be the Bridge: Pursuing God's Heart for Racial Reconciliation* (Colorado Springs: Waterbrook, 2019).
7. For more on painful messages, see chapter 7 of *Boundaries for Your*

Soul: How to Turn Your Overwhelming Thoughts and Feelings into Your Greatest Allies by Alison Cook and Kimberly Miller (Nashville: Thomas Nelson, 2018).

8. Sarah E. Hampson and Lewis R. Goldberg, "A First Large Cohort Study of Personality Trait Stability Over the 40 Years Between Elementary School and Midlife," *Journal of Personality and Social Psychology* 91, no. 4 (2006): 763–79, https://pubmed.ncbi.nlm.nih.gov/17014298/.

9. Matthew 21:12.

10. In Erikson's eight stages, you don't get to the sixth stage of intimacy until after you have resolved the first five that relate to identity. Erikson, *Childhood and Society.*

11. Psalm 139 is a great example of asking God to show you more of who you are.

12. Romans 2:4.

13. This is the argument Søren Kierkegaard made based on an exploration of John 11:4. Søren Kierkegaard, *The Sickness unto Death: A Christian Psychological Exposition for Edification and Awakening*, trans. Alastair Hannay (New York: Penguin, 1989).

Chapter 5: How Do I Find My Voice?

1. In early psychology, ego was seen as the central part of a person's psyche. According to Freud, its primary job is to mediate between what feels good (id) and what is deemed socially acceptable (superego). See Sigmund Freud, *The Ego and the Id* (New York: W. W. Norton, 1989). For more on how "ego" relates to the apostle Paul's use of the word *flesh* as the unsanctified part of us, see Richard Rohr, "Flesh and Spirit," Center for Action and Contemplation, April 6, 2018, https://cac.org/flesh-and-spirit-2018-04-06/.

2. For a detailed explanation of how to differentiate from a thought or feeling, see Alison Cook and Kimberly Miller, *Boundaries for Your Soul* (Nashville: Thomas Nelson, 2018).

3. 2 Corinthians 10:5.

4. Mark 10:13–16 THE MESSAGE.

5. Matthew 5:3–8.

6. Brené Brown, *Daring Greatly: How the Courage to Be Vulnerable Transforms the Way We Live, Love, Parent and Lead* (London: Portfolio Penguin, 2013), 75.

7. Curt Thompson, *The Soul of Shame: Retelling the Stories We Believe About Ourselves* (Downers Grove, IL: InterVarsity Press, 2015), 171–72.
8. Dan Siegel, *Mindsight: The New Science of Personal Transformation* (New York: Bantam, 2010), 137.
9. Aundi Kolber, *Try Softer: A Fresh Approach to Move Us Out of Anxiety, Stress, and Survival Mode—and into a Life of Connection and Joy* (Carol Stream, IL: Tyndale, 2020), 72.
10. Exodus 3:14.
11. Psalm 139:13–14.

Chapter 6: But Won't They Be Mad?

1. Ephesians 6:13–17.
2. For a list of counseling and support resources, visit my website, https://www.alisoncookphd.com/resources/.
3. Matthew 5:38–39.
4. N. T. Wright, *Matthew for Everyone, Part 1: Chapters 1–15* (Louisville: Westminster John Knox Press, 2004), 51–52.

Chapter 7: What If My Parents Drive Me Crazy?

1. For more on overcoming the effects of childhood wounds, see Dr. Lindsay C. Gibson, *Adult Children of Emotionally Immature Parents: How to Heal from Distant, Rejecting, or Self-Involved Parents* (Oakland, CA: New Harbinger Publications, 2015).
2. "The Good Enough Mother" is a term based on the work of D. W. Winnicott, *Playing and Reality* (1971; repr., London: Routledge Classics, 2005).
3. I'm using the term *parent* broadly to include anyone who functions as the primary caregiver for a child.
4. Psychiatrist Margaret Mahler is credited with first developing ideas about individuation and separation in the development of children. See Margaret S. Mahler, *The Psychological Birth of the Human Infant* (New York: Basic Books, 1975).
5. Parentification was first identified by Ivan Boszormenyi-Nagy and Geraldine M. Spark, *Invisible Loyalties: Reciprocity in Intergenerational Family Therapy* (New York: Harper and Row, 1973).
6. John Townsend, *The Entitlement Cure: Finding Success in Doing Hard Things the Right Way* (Grand Rapids: Zondervan, 2015).

7. Zephaniah 3:17.

8. Henri J. M. Nouwen, *The Inner Voice of Love: A Journey Through Anguish to Freedom*, repr. ed. (New York: Image, 1998).

9. Exodus 20:12.

Chapter 8: How Do I Find Friends Who Get Me?

1. For an overview of the research on dopamine, see Robert M. Sapolsky, *Behave: The Biology of Humans at Our Best and Worst* (New York: Penguin Press, 2017), 71–73. To hear Dr. Sapolsky explain this research, see "Dopamine Jackpot! Sapolsky on the Science of Pleasure," an excerpt from his Pritzker Lecture at the California Academy of Sciences given on February 15, 2011, YouTube, https://www.youtube .com/watch?v=axrywDP9Ii0.

2. C. S. Lewis, *The Four Loves* (1960; repr., New York: Harcourt Brace, 1988), 66.

3. Matthew 7:6.

4. Proverbs 13:20 ESV.

5. Oprah Winfrey, "When People Show You Who They Are, Believe Them," OWN, aired October 26, 2011, https://www.oprah.com /oprahs-lifeclass/when-people-show-you-who-they-are-believe -them-video.

6. For more on IFS, see Richard C. Schwartz, *Introduction to the Internal Family Systems Model* (Oak Park, IL: Trailhead, 2001); and Jenna Riemersma, LPC, *Altogether You: Experiencing Personal and Spiritual Transformation with Internal Family Systems Therapy* (Marietta, GA: Pivotal Press, 2020).

7. J. S. Park, *The Voices We Carry* (Chicago: Northfield, 2020), 101.

Chapter 9: Can I Get Someone to Change?

1. John Gottman, *The Seven Principles for Making Marriage Work: A Practical Guide from the Country's Foremost Relationship Expert* (New York: Harmony, 2015).

2. For more on how to create a vision for your relationship, see Harville Hendrix and Helen LaKelly Hunt, *Getting the Love You Want: A Guide for Couples* (1988; repr., New York: Holt, 2008).

3. "I" statements were first introduced by psychologist Dr. Thomas Gordon. Research shows that they are far more effective than "you"

statements when approaching conflict. For more on "I" statements see Erin Johnston, "What Are 'I Feel' Statements?," Verywell Mind, March 16, 2022, https://www.verywellmind.com/what-are-feeling-statements -425163.

4. For a detailed explanation of how to turn emotions like anger, fear, and sadness into your allies, see Cook and Miller, *Boundaries for Your Soul*.

5. Galatians 5:22–23; John 15:4.

Chapter 10: Why Doesn't God Just Fix Everything?

1. Mark 9:42.

2. Ana-Maria Rizzuto details the link between childhood experience and perceptions of God in *The Birth of the Living God: A Psychoanalytic Study* (Chicago: University of Chicago Press, 1979).

3. Mark 9:2; Luke 11:1.

4. Song of Solomon 8:6.

5. For more information about how narcissism manifests in faith communities, see Chuck DeGroat, *When Narcissism Comes to Church: Healing Your Community from Emotional and Spiritual Abuse* (Downers Grove, IL: InterVarsity Press, 2020).

6. This question is based on the ancient practice of Daily Examen that St. Ignatius of Loyola wrote about in *The Spiritual Exercises of Saint Ignatius*, trans. George E. Ganss (Chicago: Loyola Press, 1992).

7. Eugene Peterson, *Eat This Book: A Conversation in the Art of Spiritual Reading* (Grand Rapids: Eerdmans, 2006), 17.

8. Saint Teresa of Avila, *The Interior Castle* (New York: Riverhead Books, 2003), 104.

9. For an explanation of John 3:30 in its historical context, see my article on my website, "Should I Become Less?," January 20, 2022, https://www .alisoncookphd.com/should-i-become-less/.

10. Two authors who wrote beautifully about correcting this messaging are M. Robert Mulholland Jr., *The Deeper Journey: The Spirituality of Discovering Your True Self: The Sacred Call to Self Discovery* (Downers Grove, IL: InterVarsity Press, 2016); and David G. Benner, *The Gift of Being Yourself* (Downers Grove, IL: InterVarsity Press, 2015).

11. 1 Corinthians 13:11.

12. 1 Corinthians 3:2.

13. Romans 5:3–5.

14. Ephesians 4:13–16.
15. John 14:20; Psalm 139:5.
16. Proverbs 16:9.
17. Proverbs 16:3.

Chapter 11: How Will I Know I've Arrived?

1. Galatians 5:22–23.
2. Proverbs 25:15 NLT says that "soft speech can break bones."
3. John 11:26; Luke 7:19; 24:21.
4. Modeled after the famous serenity prayer by Reinhold Niebuhr.
5. These questions were adapted from the well-researched Best Possible Self exercise, in which happiness researchers found that a few moments of envisioning can increase optimism and agency. Johannes Bodo Heekerens and Michael Eid, "Inducing Positive Affect and Positive Future Expectations Using the Best-Possible-Self Intervention: A Systematic Review and Meta-Analysis," *Journal of Positive Psychology* 16, no. 7 (2020): 1–26.

About the Author

DR. ALISON COOK IS A PSYCHOLOGIST AND WRITER WHO has earned the trust of thousands of women through her practical, wise, and compassionate approach to becoming a whole person. Her popular blog and podcast reach more than 50,000 women each week. For more than two decades, she has helped women heal from past wounds, develop a strong sense of self, forge healthy relationships with others, and experience a loving God who is for them.

Originally from Wyoming, Alison studied at Dartmouth College, Denver Seminary (MA), and the University of Denver (PhD), where she specialized in the integration of theology and psychology. She is the coauthor of *Boundaries for Your Soul: How to Turn Your Overwhelming Thoughts and Feelings into Your Greatest Allies*, a faith-based adaptation of the Internal Family System (IFS) model of therapy. She and her husband, Joe, are the parents of two young adult children. Based out of Boston, they spend time in the mountains of Wyoming as often as they can. Connect with Alison at www.dralisoncook.com.